THIS DIARY BELONGS TO

....

2021 Astrology Diary

Patsy Bennett

ROCKPOOL

A Rockpool book
PO Box 252
Summer Hill
NSW 2130
Australia
rockpoolpublishing.co
Follow us! **f** 🅾 rockpoolpublishing
Tag your images with #rockpoolpublishing

ISBN 978-1-925924-30-5
Northern hemisphere edition

First published in 2020
Copyright Text © Patsy Bennett 2020
Copyright Design © Rockpool Publishing 2020
This edition published in 2020

Cover and internal design by Jessica Le, Rockpool Publishing
Edited by Lisa Macken
Typesetting by Typeskill
Frontispiece by W. G. Evans, 1856, *Map of the Constellations in July, August, September*.
Other map illustrations by Alexander Jamieson, 1822, *Celestial Atlas*.
Glyph illustrations by http://All-Silhouettes.com, Zodiac illustrations by http://vectorian.net
Compass illustration by Jessica Le, Rockpool Publishing

Printed and bound in China
10 9 8 7 6 5 4 3 2 1

NB: The planetary phenomena and aspects listed on each day are set to Greenwich Mean Time (GMT) apart from the summer time (March 28 to October 31), where they are set to British Summer Time. To convert times to your locations, please see www.timeanddate.com. Astrological interpretations take into account all aspects and the sign the sun and planets are in on each day and are not taken out of context.

Introduction

Make 2021 your best year yet! This stands to be a transformative year. Change will occur on a deep level, so if you're comfortable with change you'll love 2021. If you detest change it's important right now to plan ahead, to build a solid foundation for yourself so you feel safe as you transition into new circumstances.

This diary/planner is designed to help you to make the most of your year. If you live your life by the sun, moon and stars you'll love the *2021 Astrology Diary*: you'll have expert astrological advice right at your fingertips! I have interpreted major daily astrological data for you here in the diary pages to help you to plan ahead, so that 2021 will be all you wish it to be. Simply follow the diary dates and the interpretations of astrological phenomena will help you to be prepared and enjoy your days. (Please refer to 'How to use this diary' for more details about terminology used in the diary pages.)

The major themes for personal growth and success this year are:

- Be prepared to strategise and plan.
- Create a strong foundation in your life that will accommodate deep change.
- Be selective about what you leave behind and what you embrace.
- Socialise and network.
- Step into new terrain or reconfigure your life.
- Broaden your horizons through travel or study, and by improving relationships.
- Be patient with yourself and others and avoid aggression.

It's time to build strong foundations and yet, at the same time, you must be ready to step into fresh terrain. How is this possible, as it sounds like a contradiction in terms? And that's it right there, that's the challenge this year: how to be adaptable while also maintaining a strong foundation in your life.

Try this productive approach: begin the year by being selective and discerning about what you will let go of and what you absolutely must retain in your life. This will apply to attitudes and habits you've outgrown as much as to places and people. You may first ask: where in life can I still grow, and what do I need to let go of in order to be able to grow? And second, how will I maintain an even keel even though I am in the midst of change?

There will be areas of your life that will be the focus all year. A common theme in 2021 will be the reconfiguration of existing norms and structures in your life. For everyone, the areas that will be reconfigured will be different.

For example, for Geminis much focus will revolve around the areas in your life you share, such as duties and finances, and the bigger-picture progress you wish to achieve in life via your career and general direction. For Librans the focus will be on your personal life and home, as you find new ways to live with the people you love and the changes they experience.

The Saturn–Pluto conjunction, the effect of which will be most potent in January and then from August to December, will focus on power, authority and aggression. Whether you embrace your own power and authority or someone else's power and authority, or you resist someone's power and authority, the key to success in 2021 is to avoid aggression, as anger and aggression will only spiral into unresolved conflict.

The better your communication skills the more smoothly your year will progress. The eclipses in 2021 will span predominantly the Gemini–Sagittarius axis, suggesting that zodiac signs Gemini, Sagittarius, Pisces and Virgo will be most in line for considerable change in 2021, although all signs will be in line for an opportunity to create both a stronger structure in life and abundance.

For some all of the above will come about smoothly, but others may experience abrupt changes still to come in your life that force you to move forward into new territory. At the time such changes can appear challenging, yet in retrospect you will see there was good reason for change to have occurred.

There is a healing aspect to events in January, and this is certainly a good time to reconfigure or restructure your health routine if you feel run down or must alter your diet so it becomes more nutritious, for example.

The key to moving forward in 2021 lies in taking small, practical steps that, together, will add up to considerable change but in the day to day may not even be discernible until the final outcome occurs. For example, the benefits of a beauty or fitness regime may take time to manifest. A key to contentment this year will lie in being patient with the process of change.

You'll find out very quickly if you have forced fast results without adequate groundwork and you may then encounter obstacles. It will be far better in 2021 to be thorough with your plans rather than having to retrace your steps once obstacles arise.

A crucial pitfall in 2021 will be an unwillingness to change. You may find as a result of this that change will find you, and you will then have little say about changes that are seemingly forced upon you.

The saying 'there is nothing as sure as change' (Franklin D. Roosevelt) applies especially powerfully in February, when you may be most resistant to change or when obstacles will appear to curtail your efforts to make change. Luckily, the Aquarian new moon on February 11 should bring you in touch with people or circumstances that can help you move forward, so keep an open mind to new opportunities and be flexible.

Remarkably, March and most of April will feature no retrograde planets, making this a truly go-ahead time. This is particularly true of April, when the sun, Mercury and Venus will be in Aries until mid-month. This will be an excellent time to speed ahead with your projects, especially if you have laid solid foundations, but you must avoid risk-taking as this could land you in hot water.

May is a month of consolidation, when a healing or grounding influence will get your feet back on the ground after the speed with which events take off in March and April. Then, mid-year, retrograde Saturn and Pluto will lead the vanguard of retrograde planets that will enable you to slow down, to reassess and review your circumstances. That said, the Gemini solar eclipse on June 10 will ask that you improve your communication skills and attend to travel plans. It may be time for a fresh communications device or vehicle or simply time to learn better communication skills such as assertiveness and listening skills.

Five planets retrograde from August 20 to October 6 may make the going a little tough during fall. The eclipse season at the end of November and early December will shake up the status quo once more and, even if this causes a little disruption, events will at least move forward. If you find events are stuck or difficult in autumn, be prepared through planning and strategy and the laying of strong foundations for another growth spurt towards the end of the year.

The motto for 2021? *Be prepared.*

How to use this diary

Solar, lunar and planetary movements

This diary lists the major solar, planetary and lunar movements day by day, and I have interpreted these so you can plan your days, weeks and months according to prevailing astrological trends. You'll gain insight into which days will be favorable for your planned events – from important meetings, get togethers and celebrations to trips and life decisions; and which days will be variable, and which may even be frustrating. You'll see, when you plan your life by the stars, that sometimes taking ill-timed action can lead to disappointment and that taking well-timed action will lead to success.

The sun in the zodiac signs

Astrology is the study of the movement of celestial objects from our point of view here on earth. We are most familiar with the study of our sun signs, which depicts the movement and placement of the sun in the zodiac signs Aries through to Pisces. In the same way the sun moves through the zodiac signs Aries to Pisces through the calendar year, so do the planets and other celestial objects such as asteroid planet Chiron.

This diary features monthly forecasts when the sun is in each sign, beginning with the sun in Capricorn (December 2020 to January 2021) and proceeding through the signs and finishing once again with the sun in Capricorn in December 2021.

Each monthly forecast applies to everyone, as it is a general forecast for all sun signs. There is also a forecast uniquely for your own particular sun sign; so you'll find the 'For Capricorn' section is uniquely for Capricorns and so on. When the sun is in your own sign, this can prove particularly motivational and is a great time to get ahead with projects that resonate with your self-esteem, gut instincts and bigger-picture motivation.

The moon in the zodiac signs

Just as the sun moves through the zodiac signs, so does the moon. This diary lists these movements, as they can have a perceived influence over the mood and tone of the day, just as the sun in different signs is known to characterise different traits. So where a diary entry states: 'The moon enters Taurus', this indicates that the moon has left the zodiac sign Aries and has 'entered' the sign of Taurus, and will now reside in Taurus until it moves on to Gemini in a couple of days' time.

New moons and full moons are also listed in this diary, as these can mark turning points within your journey through the year. New moons are generally a great time to begin a new project. Full moons can signify a culmination or a peak in a project or event, so if you're planning to launch a business or your children wish to begin a new course or activity, you can check in this diary if the day you're planning your event will be favorable for beginning a fresh venture. Simply check to see if your new venture falls on or near a new moon, and also take a look at the diary entries either side of your proposed events to ensure celestial influences will be working in your favour.

Eclipses can indicate particularly powerful turning points and it is for this reason eclipses are also listed in the diary dates. If a lunar or solar eclipse is in the same sign as your own particular sun sign, it may be particularly potent.

The phases of the moon can truly influence the tone of your day, so this diary features every moon sign, daily. The moon remains in each sign approximately two days. Below, I've listed the mood depending on which sign the moon is in on a daily basis:

MOON IN ARIES: can bring an upbeat approach to life, but restlessness or fiery outbursts can result if you or those around you feel under pressure.

MOON IN TAURUS: can bring stability to feelings and routine, a sensual time and predilection for all things artistic and musical, but over-indulgence and stubbornness can result if under pressure.

MOON IN GEMINI: can bring a chatty, talkative approach to life, but flippancy, indecision and uncertainty can result if you or those around you feel under pressure.

MOON IN CANCER: a sense of security, nesting, cocooning and nurturance will be sought, for family time and those you love, but insecurities or a lack of adaptability can result if you feel under pressure.

MOON IN LEO: an upbeat approach to life and more dynamic attitude to others and yourself will arise, but a Leo moon can bring arrogance, pride and vanity to the surface if under pressure.

MOON IN VIRGO: a great time to focus on health, routine, decluttering, work and being helpful, but over-analysis, obsessive attention to detail and ambivalence can also arise if under pressure.

MOON IN LIBRA: a lovely time to focus on art, music, love, creating harmony and peace, but a sense of disharmony, indecision and dissatisfaction can arise if you're under pressure.

Moon in Scorpio: a focus on personal needs, sensuality, enjoyment of life and indulgence in all things wonderful, but if under pressure deep feelings can emerge that are intense or potentially destructive.

Moon in Sagittarius: an outgoing, upbeat phase when an adventurous attitude will bring out your joviality and lust for learning and life. When under pressure, you and others may appear blunt or disregard others' feelings.

Moon in Capricorn: can stimulate a practical and focused approach to work, to your goals and plans. But when under pressure, a sense of limitations, restrictions and authoritarian strictures can arise.

Moon in Aquarius: a quirky, outgoing phase, when trying new activities and new approaches to life will appeal. When you're under pressure, the moon in Aquarius may stimulate unreliability, unconventionality or changeability.

Moon in Pisces: a dreamy, introverted or artistic time in which music, the arts and romance will thrive. A good time for meditation. When you're under pressure, a Pisces moon can bring excessive daydreaming, forgetfulness or vagueness.

NB: If you know your moon sign, you may find that when the moon is in your sign, as listed in this diary, life is easier – or more challenging – depending on the planetary aspects to your moon at the time of your birth. Keep a note of the general mood or occurrences when the moon is in your sign and you may find that a pattern emerges.

Interplanetary aspects

Astrologers also study the movements of planets in relation to each other. The measurements are in degrees, minutes and seconds. These measurements focus on patterns and particular aspects, which are the angles between the planets, the sun and other celestial objects. This diary includes mention of these aspects between the sun and the planets, and the terminology used is explained below – from 'opposition' (when a planet is opposite another) to 'quincunx' (when a planet is at a 150-degree angle to another).

The angles the planets and the sun make to one another have meanings in astrology. For example, a 'trine' aspect (120-degree angle) can be considered beneficial for the progress of your plans; a 'square' aspect (90-degree angle) can present as a challenge (depending on your own attitude to challenges and obstacles).

By choosing dates carefully for the fruition of your plans, you will be moving forward with the benefit of the knowledge of the cosmic influences that can help your progress. NB: When you read the planetary aspects in this diary, such as 'Sun square Uranus', be aware that the aspect's influence may span to a day before and a day after the actual date it is entered in this diary, especially regarding outer planets (Neptune, Uranus and Pluto). However, the moon phases are relevant for each day.

Planetary aspects

CONJUNCTION: when a celestial object is at the same degree and generally in the same sign of the zodiac as another celestial object and therefore is aligned from our point of view here on earth. This can intensify the dynamics between the celestial objects and earth.

OPPOSITION: when a planet is opposite another, at a 180-degree angle. This can intensify the interplanetary dynamics.

SEXTILE: a 60-degree angle. This can be a peaceful, harmonious influence, or facilitate the flow of energy between planetary influences.

SEMI-SEXTILE: a 30-degree angle. This is a harmonious aspect or facilitates the flow of energy between planetary influences.

SQUARE: a 90-degree angle. This can be a challenging aspect, but as some people get going when the going gets tough it can lead to a breakthrough.

TRINE: a 120-degree angle. This can be a peaceful, harmonious influence, or facilitate the flow of energy between planetary influences.

QUINCUNX: a 150-degree angle. This can present a hurdle to be overcome.

Retrogrades

Planets can appear to go backwards, from our point of view here on earth. The best-known retrograde phases are those of Mercury and Venus, although all other planets also turn retrograde and these retrograde phases are also mentioned in this diary. Retrograde phases can be a good time to assimilate, consolidate and integrate recent developments, although traditionally retrograde phases are associated with delays, a slow down or difficult process. For example, a Mercury retrograde phase is often associated with difficult communications or traffic snarls, and yet it can be an excellent time to integrate events and to consolidate, review and re-order your ideas. This diary lists start – and finish – dates of Mercury retrograde phases, as well as the kinds of activities that may be influenced by this phenomenon and in the same sign of the zodiac.

A 'station' is when planets 'turn' from one direction to the other from our point of view here on earth.

Amuret Vulpecula
THE FOX & GOOSE R.300.D.25

β Albireo
ι Anser

Delphinus
DOLPHIN
R.308.D.15

Sagitta
THE ARROW

CERBERUS

COLURE

Maaye

THE EAGLE

R.ds D.s.

Deneb el Okab

Ras Alhague

cb el Delphini

Janzed

Ras Alhague

Albain

Taurus of
PONIATOWSKI
R.300V

Rudiain

Var.

EQUINOCTIAL

ANTINOUS

SOLSTITIAL

THE

Nilotica

Scutum Sobieski
SOBIESKIS SHIELD

rma

D

Giedi

Sagittarius
THE ARCHER
R.285.D.33

THE EARTHS ORBIT

OR ECLIPTIC

Corn us

Trebellum

THE

OAT

Lesui

Corona Australis
THE SOUTH CROWN

α Ruchball to Ramih

β Alab ur Ramih

le of Magnitudes

2021 NORTHERN HEMISPHERE MOON PHASES

JANUARY

S	M	T	W	T	F	S
31					1	2
3	4	5	6	7	8	9
10	11	12	13	14	15	16
17	18	19	20	21	22	23
24	25	26	27	28	29	30

FEBRUARY

S	M	T	W	T	F	S
	1	2	3	4	5	6
7	8	9	10	11	12	13
14	15	16	17	18	19	20
21	22	23	24	25	26	27
28						

MARCH

S	M	T	W	T	F	S
	1	2	3	4	5	6
7	8	9	10	11	12	13
14	15	16	17	18	19	20
21	22	23	24	25	26	27
28	29	30	31			

APRIL

S	M	T	W	T	F	S
				1	2	3
4	5	6	7	8	9	10
11	12	13	14	15	16	17
18	19	20	21	22	23	24
25	26	27	28	29	30	

MAY

S	M	T	W	T	F	S
30	31					1
2	3	4	5	6	7	8
9	10	11	12	13	14	15
16	17	18	19	20	21	22
23	24	25	26	27	28	29

JUNE

S	M	T	W	T	F	S
		1	2	3	4	5
6	7	8	9	10	11	12
13	14	15	16	17	18	19
20	21	22	23	24	25	26
27	28	29	30			

2021 NORTHERN HEMISPHERE MOON PHASES

JULY

S	M	T	W	T	F	S
				1	2	3
				●	◗	◖
4	5	6	7	8	9	10
◖	◖	◖	◖	◖	◖	○
11	12	13	14	15	16	17
◗	◗	◗	◗	◗	◗	◗
18	19	20	21	22	23	24
●	●	●	●	●	●	●
25	26	27	28	29	30	31
●	●	●	●	◗	◖	◖

AUGUST

S	M	T	W	T	F	S
1	2	3	4	5	6	7
◖	◖	◖	◖	◖	◖	◖
8	9	10	11	12	13	14
○	◗	◗	◗	◗	◗	◗
15	16	17	18	19	20	21
◗	◗	●	●	●	●	●
22	23	24	25	26	27	28
●	●	●	●	●	●	◗
29	30	31				
●	◗	◖				

SEPTEMBER

S	M	T	W	T	F	S
			1	2	3	4
			◖	◖	◖	◖
5	6	7	8	9	10	11
◖	◖	○	◗	◗	◗	◗
12	13	14	15	16	17	18
◗	◗	●	●	●	●	●
19	20	21	22	23	24	25
●	●	●	●	●	●	●
26	27	28	29	30		
◖	●	●	●	◗		

OCTOBER

S	M	T	W	T	F	S
31					1	2
◖					◖	◖
3	4	5	6	7	8	9
◖	◖	◖	○	◗	◗	◗
10	11	12	13	14	15	16
◗	◗	◗	◗	◗	●	●
17	18	19	20	21	22	23
●	●	●	●	●	●	●
24	25	26	27	28	29	30
◖	●	◖	◖	◖	◖	◖

NOVEMBER

S	M	T	W	T	F	S
	1	2	3	4	5	6
	◖	◖	◖	○	◗	◗
7	8	9	10	11	12	13
◗	◗	◗	◗	◗	◗	●
14	15	16	17	18	19	20
●	●	●	●	●	●	●
21	22	23	24	25	26	27
●	●	◖	◖	◖	◖	◖
28	29	30				
◖	◖	◖				

DECEMBER

S	M	T	W	T	F	S
			1	2	3	4
			◖	◖	◖	○
5	6	7	8	9	10	11
◗	◗	◗	◗	◗	◗	◗
12	13	14	15	16	17	18
◗	●	●	●	●	●	●
19	20	21	22	23	24	25
●	●	●	●	●	◗	◖
26	27	28	29	30	31	
◖	◖	◖	◖	◖	◖	

○ New moon   ● Full moon

January 2021

The sun entered Capricorn, December 21, 2020

The potent full moon at the end of 2020 puts a punctuation mark on the end of that year, illuminating areas in your life you'd like to develop and those you are more inclined to leave behind. In January 2021 you may already feel ready to put many ideas and projects onto a more solid platform. The Capricorn new moon on January 13 will conjunct Pluto, the dwarf planet associated with transformation, and loosely conjunct Mercury, Saturn and Jupiter in Aquarius, signalling that much of the transformation this year will revolve around new turf, new ideas, growth and expansion.

Venus, the planet of love, beauty and money, will be in Sagittarius until January 8, helping you to be adventurous in the key areas of romance, well-being and finances. And, just as Venus steps into Capricorn on January 9, the planet of beauty will 'trine' Mars, signalling this as an excellent time to put form to your plans concerning love and money and to take adventurous steps forward. The proviso here is that you do adequate research, especially if you're entering new terrain via fresh projects or ties.

You'll find out quickly mid-January if you have over- or under-estimated your circumstances and, while a challenge may arise if this is so, you will nevertheless gain the opportunity to set things straight once more. To truly break new ground in 2021, you need to have faith and trust that your preparation and research will be sufficient. Subsequently, a leap of faith will be the conduit to your success, leading to a considerable sense of fulfilment when your efforts pay off.

For Capricorns

The full moon at the end of 2020 will place focus firmly on nurturance and how to be more caring, both of self and the people you love. If you overworked in 2020, a beneficial resolution for you in 2021 will be to find more time for family, for friends – and for yourself.

The Capricorn new moon on January 13 will coincide with a tough aspect between your sign's ruler Saturn and assertive Mars; an unpredictable person or circumstance could fire up at this time. And, while this astrological aspect may be a challenge or will involve hard work at the least, it will also provide the incentive to effectively smooth the way forward for you and for those you love for the rest of the year.

Look for solutions to problems and find answers rather than fan the flames of conflict, as the more proactive and willing you are to build better circumstances in your life the better for you. If you have already been working on providing a stronger platform for yourself throughout 2020, you may find that January will present you with a considerable breakthrough and success.

INTENTIONS *for the* YEAR

MONDAY 28

TUESDAY 29

WEDNESDAY 30

THURSDAY 31

FRIDAY 1 ●

Mercury sextile Neptune: this is a dreamy start to the new year. If you over-indulged last night you may feel a little disorientated today. Nevertheless, romance could blossom. Moon in Leo.

SATURDAY 2 ●

Moon in Leo.

SUNDAY 3 ●

Moon in Virgo.

			JANUARY			
S	M	T	W	T	F	S
					1	2
3	4	5	6	7	8	9
10	11	12	13	14	15	16
17	18	19	20	21	22	23
24	25	26	27	28	29	30
31						

MONDAY 4

Venus semi-sextile Pluto; Mercury conjunct Pluto: you may hear important news. Romance and love could flourish, although you or someone close may experience particularly strong emotions. Moon in Virgo.

TUESDAY 5

Moon in Libra.

WEDNESDAY 6

Mars enters Taurus: you may feel increasingly inclined to follow your passions and to indulge in the good things in life over the next two months. Moon in Libra.

THURSDAY 7

Mercury semi-sextile Venus: this is a good day to talk, for romance and for financial transactions, but you must avoid rash decisions. Moon in Scorpio.

FRIDAY 8 ☾

Venus enters Capricorn; Mercury enters Aquarius; sun sextile Neptune: developments may put a new perspective on your projects and plans. Be open to new ideas. You'll enjoy indulging in your favorite activities. Romance, music and creativity could flourish. Moon in Scorpio.

SATURDAY 9 ☾

Moon enters Sagittarius.

SUNDAY 10 ☾

Venus trine Mars; Venus semi-sextile Saturn: creativity, love, romance, money and get togethers will focus your mind on what – and who – truly matters. Romance could blossom, so plan a treat! Moon in Sagittarius.

			JANUARY			
S	M	T	W	T	F	S
					1	2
3	4	5	6	7	8	9
10	11	12	13	14	15	16
17	18	19	20	21	22	23
24	25	26	27	28	29	30
31						

MONDAY 11   (

Mercury conjunct Jupiter: a trip, chat or communications could be
decisive, so ensure you gain all the information you need to succeed.
Moon enters Capricorn.

TUESDAY 12   (

Mercury square Uranus; Venus semi-sextile Jupiter: a surprise is on the way.
You may gain a sense of accomplishment but must avoid misunderstandings.
Back up computers and plan ahead to avoid travel delays. Moon in Capricorn.

WEDNESDAY 13   ○

New moon in Capricorn; Mars square Saturn: this is an excellent time to put in
place a careful plan of action for success. Avoid making rash decisions but also
be prepared to take steps forward innovatively and courageously. Moon enters
Aquarius in the evening.

THURSDAY 14   )

Uranus ends its retrograde phase; sun conjunct Pluto; Venus trine Uranus: the
period just after the new moon is generally a good time to begin new projects
and bravely move forward. You may experience intense developments now, so
ensure you take things step by step. A surprise may arise for some regarding
money; for others, love. Moon in Aquarius.

FRIDAY 15)

Moon enters Pisces.

SATURDAY 16)

Moon in Pisces.

SUNDAY 17)

Moon in Pisces.

			JANUARY			
S	M	T	W	T	F	S
					1	2
3	4	5	6	7	8	9
10	11	12	13	14	15	16
17	18	19	20	21	22	23
24	25	26	27	28	29	30
31						

January to February 2021

Sun enters Aquarius, January 19

The sun will join Saturn, Jupiter and Mercury in Aquarius, which spells a particularly exciting time especially if you are open to change and advancement into new and untested territory. If you prefer the status quo, the next four weeks may represent a roller coaster – at least from now until Mercury turns retrograde at the end of January. In February, you'll gain the opportunity to reassess and review circumstances.

The full moon in Leo on January 28 will be a call to action, especially in areas you have been reluctant to change for fear of upsetting present circumstances. The call to action will be hard to ignore, as your deeper emotions may come to the surface. After this full moon you will effectively be able to look forward to a more healing and therapeutic scenario.

Once Venus joins the sun, Mercury, Saturn and Jupiter in Aquarius from February 1 onwards, you may gain an increasing sense of being engaged in your activities as you deepen your understanding of the value of current developments, especially in connection with new ventures and projects.

The success of your endeavours will lie in being focused on allowing new dynamics to enter your everyday life, and in building a strong infrastructure so they might thrive.

Important discussions during the second week of February will determine many of your decisions; ensure you research well at this time to avoid misdirection. A key circumstance that can broaden your horizons involving travel, study, legal or spiritual matters, for example, and with someone special may be a determining factor. Keep an open mind as developments towards February 19 will illuminate your true feelings about prospective changes. Be guided, as always, by your wish for peace, kindness and harmony.

For Aquarians

You will gain a sense of freedom and liberation, making 2021 a big year for you. If you are not ready for it you may feel overwhelmed by change and subsequently may choose to avoid the opportunities that come your way.

There will be four planets and the sun in Aquarius from February 1, putting the focus firmly on your own personal life. Mercury will be retrograde in your sign from January 30 until February 21, enabling you to choose your activities carefully now and embrace something new. However, you may feel inner tension during February, wishing to move ahead yet fearing the consequences. You must base decisions on your wisdom and experience while simultaneously welcoming the new. Otherwise, inner tension may be a stumbling block.

Luckily, the Aquarian new moon on February 11 will provide you with the impulse and insight to instigate fresh projects, and to make valid decisions in your personal life through to March and April. These will be ideal months to set sail on a fresh course in whichever field has inspired you and caught your imagination during the four weeks from January to February while the sun is in your sign.

MONDAY 18 ☽

Jupiter square Uranus: you may be surprised by a development. Avoid a rash reaction, but be prepared to find a solution to problems that arise. Moon in Aries.

TUESDAY 19 ☽

The sun enters Aquarius: the next four weeks will bring your imagination out and also your inventiveness. You may feel more adventurous and ready to develop your projects. Moon in Aries.

WEDNESDAY 20 ☽

Mercury semi-sextile Neptune; Mars conjunct Uranus: think outside the square and be adaptable. You may experience an unexpected development or may be ready to begin something new. Ensure you have all the facts. Moon enters Taurus.

THURSDAY 21 ☽

Moon in Taurus.

FRIDAY 22

Moon in Taurus.

SATURDAY 23

Venus sextile Neptune; Mars square Jupiter: your plans may come up against a challenge, but if they are realistic and based on research and practicalities you could excel. Avoid impulsiveness. Romance could flourish as long as you avoid taking someone for granted. Moon enters Gemini.

SUNDAY 24

Sun conjunct Saturn: a clever plan could come together. You'll enjoy a reunion, although there may be a level of unpredictability about events this weekend. Avoid stubbornness; be flexible. Moon in Gemini.

| | | JANUARY | | | | |
S	M	T	W	T	F	S
					1	2
3	4	5	6	7	8	9
10	11	12	13	14	15	16
17	18	19	20	21	22	23
24	25	26	27	28	29	30
31						

MONDAY 25 ●

Sun sextile Chiron: there is a therapeutic aspect to the day; it is a good day for a health appointment and to seek advice from an expert. Moon enters Cancer.

TUESDAY 26 ●

Sun square Uranus; Mercury semi-sextile Pluto: you can achieve a great deal through research, good communication skills and by thinking outside the square, but must avoid impulsiveness and limiting your options. Moon in Cancer.

WEDNESDAY 27 ●

Moon in Cancer.

THURSDAY 28 ●

Full moon in Leo; Venus conjunct Pluto: love and romance could blossom, but so, too, could intense emotions, some of which may be destructive. Avoid tempers and arguments, as they are likely to spiral. Moon in Leo.

FRIDAY 29 ●

Sun conjunct Jupiter; Mercury semi-sextile Venus: there may be a larger-than-life quality about events. Be adventurous, but avoid pushing for results and throwing caution to the wind. Moon in Leo.

SATURDAY 30 ●

Mercury begins a retrograde phase: try to get important communications and loose ends tied up as communications and travel may be a little delayed or mixed over the next few weeks. Moon enters Virgo.

SUNDAY 31 ●

Moon in Virgo.

JANUARY

S	M	T	W	T	F	S
					1	2
3	4	5	6	7	8	9
10	11	12	13	14	15	16
17	18	19	20	21	22	23
24	25	26	27	28	29	30
31						

MONDAY 1

Venus enters Aquarius; sun square Mars: watch tempers and tantrums today. Pace yourself and aim to defuse tension when you can. You could excel with a careful approach and ingenuity. You may be drawn to exciting new ventures over the coming weeks. Moon enters Libra.

TUESDAY 2

Moon in Libra.

WEDNESDAY 3

Mercury semi-sextile Pluto: this is a good day to review and reassess some of your decisions and communications. You may enjoy a reunion. Moon enters Scorpio.

THURSDAY 4

Moon in Scorpio.

FRIDAY 5 ◖

Moon enters Sagittarius.

SATURDAY 6 ◖

Venus conjunct Saturn; Venus sextile Chiron: this is a good day to make agreements, although you may need to compromise or reach a mutually agreeable outcome. There is a therapeutic quality about events, even if strong feelings arise. Moon in Sagittarius.

SUNDAY 7 ◖

Venus square Uranus: circumstances may surprise you this weekend or will be out of the ordinary. Be open-minded and adaptable for the best results. Moon enters Capricorn.

		FEBRUARY				
S	M	T	W	T	F	S
	1	2	3	4	5	6
7	8	9	10	11	12	13
14	15	16	17	18	19	20
21	22	23	24	25	26	27
28						

MONDAY 8 ☽

Sun conjunct Mercury; sun semi-sextile Neptune: this is a good day for romance, the arts and creativity. A trip or news may be significant. At work you may be forgetful or idealistic, so ensure you focus harder than usual. Moon in Capricorn.

TUESDAY 9 ☽

Mercury semi-sextile Neptune; Chiron sextile Saturn: you may feel inspired and wish to discuss your long-term plans with someone special. Avoid idealism and combine your imagination with practicalities. This may be a therapeutic day. Moon in Capricorn.

WEDNESDAY 10 ☽

Mercury square Mars: developments may occur rapidly and you may feel restless. Avoid impulsiveness and impatience. Choose words carefully and you could attain a goal. Moon enters Aquarius.

THURSDAY 11 ○

New moon in Aquarius; Venus conjunct Jupiter: be prepared to consider new ideas and projects. This is a good time to set innovative and upbeat projects in motion. Be spontaneous but avoid rash decisions. News regarding love or money may arise. A trip could be a turning point. Love could flourish.

FRIDAY 12)

Moon enters Pisces.

SATURDAY 13)

Mercury conjunct Venus: you may enjoy a reunion or will receive news you have been waiting for, especially to do with love or money. It's a good day to review your circumstances. Moon in Pisces.

SUNDAY 14)

Mercury conjunct Jupiter; Mars sextile Neptune: happy St Valentine's Day! This is a super romantic day astrologically this year, so be bold and enjoy love through the language of romance: flowers, candles, chocolate and sweet words. Moon enters Aries.

		FEBRUARY				
S	M	T	W	T	F	S
	1	2	3	4	5	6
7	8	9	10	11	12	13
14	15	16	17	18	19	20
21	22	23	24	25	26	27
28						

february to march 2021

Sun enters Pisces, February 18

As the sun enters Pisces it leaves behind four planets in Aquarius, so the strong Aquarian energy that has pervaded the past month will persist, even with the sun in Pisces. And with feisty Mars at a tense angle with love planet Venus, there may be tension galore as fresh ideas, projects and, for some, obstacles must be negotiated.

The prevailing Saturn square Uranus aspect will highlight areas you feel stuck in yet reluctant to change. Consider your true aims, values and priorities to orientate your thoughts. Luckily, Mercury will end its retrograde phase on February 22, helping communications and gradually enabling carefully laid plans to gain momentum over the coming months.

Mars trine Pluto on February 25 characterises the upcoming weeks: excellent opportunities to put your plans in motion, and also to seek deeper understanding of someone special (especially for earth signs) and to find more stability in an ever-changing world.

The Virgo full moon on February 27 will offer a great opportunity to fine-tune plans and to focus on details. You may also wish to collaborate with someone in particular or to enter new territory.

Ensure you are on the same page as those you make plans with and, if not, decide if this is something you can live with or if you must seek fresh direction. March has no planets retrograde, so you are likely to steam ahead with well-laid plans.

For Pisces

Even while the sun will be in your sign for the next four weeks, there is every chance you feel slightly like a fish out of water initially due to the plethora of planets in Aquarius. Once Venus joins the sun in your sign on February 25, you'll appreciate the increasing sense of relative ease with which events begin to move ahead. At this time you may even experience a pleasant development that provides a sense of direction and fulfilment. But if this is a challenging time for you, it will be important to establish a reliable health and wellness regime to ensure you are supporting yourself on a constitutional level.

The full moon in Virgo on February 27 will signal a fresh chapter for you in a partnership or collaboration – predominantly for February Pisces – and at work or within your daily routine for March Fish. This will also be a good time for all Fish to consider a health overhaul: to look at your diet and exercise regime from a new perspective.

When Venus sextiles Uranus on March 3 you may receive unexpectedly good news, or will at the least glimpse the chance of a breakthrough if matters have been stuck.

Developments towards March 9 will clarify how you feel about an artistic or creative project or romance. You may find yourself at odds with someone, in which case you may need to double check that each of your values align.

The Pisces new moon on March 13 will provide incentive to launch new ideas. This may also be a particularly romantic time.

MONDAY 15 ☽

Moon in Aries.

TUESDAY 16 ☽

Moon in Aries.

WEDNESDAY 17 ☽

Venus semi-sextile Neptune; Saturn square Uranus: this is another romantic day, so why not organise a treat or a get together? Your plans may progress, but you must be practical and willing to go beyond your comfort zone. Be careful with details. Moon enters Taurus.

THURSDAY 18 ☽

Sun enters Pisces: an inspiring time awaits. Moon in Taurus.

FRIDAY 19 ◗

Venus square Mars: strong emotions are best channelled into constructive pursuits. Avoid arguments; look for common ground and research your ideas thoroughly. Be prepared to move forward into new areas. Moon enters Gemini.

SATURDAY 20 ◗

Moon in Gemini.

SUNDAY 21 ◗

Moon in Gemini.

FEBRUARY

S	M	T	W	T	F	S
	1	2	3	4	5	6
7	8	9	10	11	12	13
14	15	16	17	18	19	20
21	22	23	24	25	26	27
28						

MONDAY 22

Mercury ends its retrograde phase; Venus semi-sextile Pluto: you can gradually move ahead with your various plans and projects, although news may first arrive that sets things in perspective. Romance could flourish, and strong emotions may arise. Moon in Cancer.

TUESDAY 23

Moon in Cancer.

WEDNESDAY 24

Moon enters Leo.

THURSDAY 25

Sun sextile Uranus; Mars trine Pluto: this is a high-energy day. For some it will be motivational, but for others a little overwhelming. Aim to channel energy into your favorite activities and to get chores done. Expect a surprise. Moon in Leo.

FRIDAY 26 ●

Moon enters Virgo.

SATURDAY 27 ●

Full moon in Virgo: this is a good day to get organised and to plan ahead, especially regarding a reunion, trip or fun project.

SUNDAY 28 ●

Moon enters Libra.

		FEBRUARY				
S	M	T	W	T	F	S
	1	2	3	4	5	6
7	8	9	10	11	12	13
14	15	16	17	18	19	20
21	22	23	24	25	26	27
28						

MONDAY 1 ●

Moon in Libra.

TUESDAY 2 ●

Moon enters Scorpio.

WEDNESDAY 3 ●

Venus sextile Uranus: you may experience a surprise. An impromptu get together may be pleasant. Moon in Scorpio.

THURSDAY 4 ●

Mars enters Gemini; Venus semi-sextile Saturn: your projects and plans can move forward now. Matters that have been stuck could free up with good planning. Moon in Scorpio.

FRIDAY 5 ◖

Moon in Sagittarius.

SATURDAY 6 ◖

Moon in Sagittarius.

SUNDAY 7 ◖

Moon in Capricorn.

		MARCH				
S	M	T	W	T	F	S
	1	2	3	4	5	6
7	8	9	10	11	12	13
14	15	16	17	18	19	20
21	22	23	24	25	26	27
28	29	30	31			

MONDAY 8 ☽

Sun semi-sextile Jupiter; Mercury semi-sextile Neptune: this is a lovely day for making plans for travel, romance and creativity. Moon in Capricorn.

TUESDAY 9 ☽

Venus square the moon's nodes: you may be at odds with someone, and the clearer you are with communications the better in the long-term. Moon enters Aquarius.

WEDNESDAY 10 ☽

Moon in Aquarius.

THURSDAY 11 ☽

Moon enters Pisces.

FRIDAY 12   (

Moon in Pisces.

SATURDAY 13   ○

New moon in Pisces: a good time to consider your dreams and place your intention to involve more art, romance and creativity in your life. Moon enters Aries late at night.

SUNDAY 14   )

Venus conjunct Neptune: a most romantic time; art and creativity will flourish at this time. Avoid disappointment by checking details, as mistakes could be made. Moon in Aries.

		MARCH				
S	M	T	W	T	F	S
	1	2	3	4	5	6
7	8	9	10	11	12	13
14	15	16	17	18	19	20
21	22	23	24	25	26	27
28	29	30	31			

march to april 2021

Sun enters Aries, March 20

As the sun enters Aries this marks the spring equinox, a time when your plans and projects can gain momentum as the seeds you have sown so far this year begin to grow.

This is another zodiacal month with no planets retrograde so it's all systems go. If you prefer life to be at a gentler pace, it's important to take measures to slow things down to avoid feeling you're in a whirl.

Fire and air signs may feel particularly in your element now and could profit from the fast pace. However, if you feel caught up in others' dramas or tend to be reluctant to make changes in life, this is the month to work on developing a thicker skin (while still being perceptive) and to develop a more adaptable approach to life, or else you could feel disorientated by developments.

The full moon in Libra on March 28 will align opposite Chiron and Venus, suggesting important developments in your love life, health or creativity. An amazing kite formation with the sun, Venus and Chiron at the apex suggests important decisions now are best navigated carefully, as you could certainly make changes in your life.

The full moon will encourage you to strive for balance and harmony, and to take decisive action to build a strong platform for happiness in your life. Your efforts in this respect are likely to take – if not immediately, then incrementally over the next few months.

For Aries

Both the sun and Venus will be in Aries, and there will be no planets retrograde. This scenario equals a month made in heaven for you as you will feel dynamic and success could be yours. The major pitfall, however, will be taking on too much and overwhelming yourself, so it's important you pace yourself despite such fertile ground for progress and happiness. A strong link with your past or with someone from your past will characterise key developments this month.

The full moon on March 28 will focus your mind on what – and who – is truly important to you, right across the board from work to money and people. If you experience a dip in self-esteem or even a disappointment at this time, rest assured a constructive approach to new territory and setting fresh boundaries will lead to healing, self-discovery and a positive outcome.

The Aries new moon on April 12 will spotlight key decisions in your life that may even spell a new direction. Aim for the most therapeutic and healing options. Unless you are absolutely confident your ventures will work, they could prove more challenging than you hope.

MARCH

MONDAY 15)

Moon in Aries.

TUESDAY 16)

Sun sextile Pluto: you can make great headway with your projects and plans. It's a good day to make changes. Moon enters Taurus.

WEDNESDAY 17)

Moon in Taurus.

THURSDAY 18)

Venus sextile Pluto; Mars sextile Chiron: a good day to give your projects a gentle push and to avoid not taking 'no' for an answer. Moon enters Gemini.

FRIDAY 19 ◗

Moon in Gemini.

SATURDAY 20 ◗

Sun enters Aries; spring equinox: this is a period of growth and a good time to nurture new plans and ideas. Moon in Gemini.

SUNDAY 21 ◗

Venus enters Aries; Mercury sextile Uranus: you may be surprised by developments today. Words will flow, although developments may be out of the ordinary. Moon enters Cancer.

		MARCH				
S	M	T	W	T	F	S
	1	2	3	4	5	6
7	8	9	10	11	12	13
14	15	16	17	18	19	20
21	22	23	24	25	26	27
28	29	30	31			

MONDAY 22

Mars trine Saturn: this is an excellent day to put your plans in motion and to find a level of strategy and foundation in your projects. Moon in Cancer.

TUESDAY 23

Mercury semi-sextile Saturn: a good day to talk and for negotiations. Financial matters may improve. Avoid rash decisions. Moon enters Leo.

WEDNESDAY 24

Mercury square Mars: you may be talking at cross purposes with someone. Avoid taking random comments personally, but if making important decisions ensure you have all the facts. Moon in Leo.

THURSDAY 25

Moon in Leo.

FRIDAY 26 ●

Sun conjunct Venus; Mars conjunct moon's north node: a good day for the arts, for romance and for getting in touch with someone important at work and at home. You may meet or hear from someone from out of the blue. Avoid rash decisions; do your research. Moon in Virgo.

SATURDAY 27 ●

Moon in Virgo.

SUNDAY 28 ●

Full moon in Libra; Venus semi-sextile Uranus: this full moon may include a surprise and you will wish to establish more peace and harmony in your life as you move forward.

		MARCH				
S	M	T	W	T	F	S
	1	2	3	4	5	6
7	8	9	10	11	12	13
14	15	16	17	18	19	20
21	22	23	24	25	26	27
28	29	30	31			

MONDAY 29 ●

Sun semi-sextile Uranus: expect a surprise. Moon in Libra.

TUESDAY 30 ●

Mercury conjunct Neptune; Venus sextile Saturn: this is a good day for inspiration, the arts and to develop your spirituality. Financial matters may flow. However, forgetfulness and daydreaming may also arise, so be super-focused. Moon in Scorpio.

WEDNESDAY 31 ●

Sun sextile Saturn: this is a good day to get organised, to make a commitment or an agreement and for getting work done. Moon in Scorpio.

THURSDAY 1 ●

Moon in Sagittarius.

FRIDAY 2

Sun sextile moon's north node; Mercury sextile Pluto: a good day for get togethers; you may hear from an old friend. Moon in Sagittarius.

SATURDAY 3

Moon enters Capricorn.

SUNDAY 4

Moon in Capricorn.

		APRIL				
S	M	T	W	T	F	S
				1	2	3
4	5	6	7	8	9	10
11	12	13	14	15	16	17
18	19	20	21	22	23	24
25	26	27	28	29	30	

MONDAY 5 ☾

Moon enters Aquarius.

TUESDAY 6 ☾

Venus sextile Mars: a good day for romance, meetings and negotiations, especially if you're ready for change. Moon in Aquarius.

WEDNESDAY 7 ☾

Moon enters Pisces.

THURSDAY 8 ☾

Venus semi-sextile Neptune; Chiron semi-sextile Uranus: art, music, dance and creativity will appeal. Romance could flourish. Someone may need your help unexpectedly or vice versa; support will be available. Moon in Pisces.

FRIDAY 9   (

Mars square Neptune: you may feel particularly romantic, idealistic and creative but must avoid snap decisions and making assumptions. Moon in Pisces.

SATURDAY 10   (

Mercury sextile Saturn; Venus sextile Jupiter: this is a good day for meetings and making agreements and for being adventurous. You'll enjoy being spontaneous but will regret hasty decisions. Moon in Aries.

SUNDAY 11   (

Sun semi-sextile Neptune: a lovely day for art, movies, romance, relaxation and fun, so organise a treat! Moon in Aries.

		APRIL				
S	M	T	W	T	F	S
				1	2	3
4	5	6	7	8	9	10
11	12	13	14	15	16	17
18	19	20	21	22	23	24
25	26	27	28	29	30	

MONDAY 12   ○

New moon in Aries; Venus square Pluto: this is a good day to set a new project or plan in motion, especially if you have already done considerable research. You must avoid conflict, as it may quickly escalate and become long term. Avoid snap decisions. Moon enters Taurus in the evening.

TUESDAY 13   )

Sun sextile Mars: you can accomplish a great deal but must guard against impulsiveness. Moon in Taurus.

WEDNESDAY 14   )

Moon in Taurus.

THURSDAY 15   )

Sun sextile Jupiter; Mercury semi-sextile Neptune: an optimistic frame of mind will accomplish great feats. Creative and artistic, sporty and imaginative past-times may feel particularly inspiring today. Moon in Gemini.

FRIDAY 16 ❯

Sun square Pluto: you may feel motivated by a belief or passion but must guard against zeal and conflict. Events may rake up feelings relating back to last weekend; be prepared to change and to instigate long-term plans if necessary. Moon in Gemini.

SATURDAY 17 ❯

Mercury sextile Jupiter; Mercury sextile Mars; Mercury square Pluto; Mars trine Jupiter: a good day to make great progress and to initiate plans, but you must be realistic and practical and avoid making unnecessary waves or initiating conflict. Moon enters Cancer.

SUNDAY 18 ❯

Mars quincunx Pluto: rise to challenges today; developments will merit careful communications and then you could excel. Avoid stepping on someone's toes and impulsiveness. Moon in Cancer.

APRIL

S	M	T	W	T	F	S
				1	2	3
4	5	6	7	8	9	10
11	12	13	14	15	16	17
18	19	20	21	22	23	24
25	26	27	28	29	30	

April to May 2021

Sun enters Taurus, April 19

This zodiacal month can best be described as 'variable', and you will see at the Scorpio full moon supermoon on April 27 whether you must reinstate the status quo due to prevailing winds of change.

Early May will feature a roller-coaster ride unless you already have a strong foundation and goals you are keen to pursue. The series of trines to Pluto present a changeable scenario you are best to anticipate by planning to take things step by step. You may feel the need for change in your life but must weigh your options carefully.

Once Jupiter steps into Pisces on May 13 you may feel inspired to learn a new skill, to travel or to deepen your understanding of life, spirituality and yourself. You may, however, feel initially overwhelmed by developments. If the latter, slow down. Jupiter in Pisces will give you a taste of what is to come from 2022 over the next two years, so you will have plenty of time to develop new ideas. Be prepared nevertheless to enter new territory.

Once Venus enters Gemini on May 9 you may feel more light-hearted or even ambivalent. Indecision may arise, and so you must trust that your values and principles will guide you about key matters over the coming weeks.

For Taureans

The alignment of the sun, Mercury, Venus and Uranus in Taurus spells a busy time, and one that will include a surprise or two. You may need to rethink, re-order or regroup, and this most especially in connection with finances or your personal life.

Help is at hand; it will be a case of asking for assistance. Do not be afraid to reach back into the past and ask your supporters to help out if it is needed. You may even be surprised by where your support comes from now.

The Scorpio full moon and supermoon on April 27 will offer you the chance to put in place beneficial changes in your personal life, work and health routines, but hard work will be necessary. You may even be surprised by news that is a catalyst for change.

Early May has a decidedly stop-start, up-down tone. Be ready to innovate, to change your activities and mindset in line with developments. The more adaptable you can be during this month the better for you, while at the same time maintaining clear sight of your goals. Sounds paradoxical? It is, but then success often depends on walking the fine line between dogged determination and flexibility.

The Taurus new moon on May 11 will signal a fresh chapter for you in your personal life and, for some, at work. It will be a good time to make long-overdue changes.

MONDAY 19 ◗

Sun enters Taurus; sun conjunct Mercury: you may receive important news. A trip may be decisive. Moon in Cancer.

TUESDAY 20 ◗

Jupiter semi-sextile Pluto; Chiron semi-sextile Uranus: your plans could take a turn for the better, but if they take a turn for the worse it's important to make changes sooner rather than later. Moon enters Leo.

WEDNESDAY 21 ◗

Moon in Leo.

THURSDAY 22 ●

Moon in Virgo.

FRIDAY 23 ●

Venus conjunct Uranus: be prepared for a surprise or a fresh development that takes you into new terrain. Moon in Virgo.

SATURDAY 24 ●

Mercury conjunct Uranus: you may receive unexpected news. A trip may take you into new territory. You may enjoy revisiting a past experience. A financial matter will deserve careful appraisal. Moon enters Libra.

SUNDAY 25 ●

Venus square Saturn; Mercury square Saturn: take a moment to unwind. You may feel sensitive or stubborn. A financial or personal matter deserves careful focus. Adopt an open mind and, if someone is obstinate, look for a way ahead without arguments. Moon in Libra.

				APRIL		
S	M	T	W	T	F	S
				1	2	3
4	5	6	7	8	9	10
11	12	13	14	15	16	17
18	19	20	21	22	23	24
25	26	27	28	29	30	

MONDAY 26 ●

Mercury conjunct Venus: important talks or a trip will be relevant now; it's a good time to consider your circumstances step by step. Moon enters Scorpio.

TUESDAY 27 ●

Full moon supermoon in Scorpio: you may feel passionate about your ideas and wishes. The full moon may illuminate where you will benefit from a more flexible attitude.

WEDNESDAY 28 ●

Moon enters Sagittarius.

THURSDAY 29 ●

Moon in Sagittarius.

FRIDAY 30 ●

Sun conjunct Uranus; Mercury sextile Neptune: discussions and plans may be easier to negotiate than recently but you must rely on the facts, not supposition. You may be surprised by developments or news. Moon enters Capricorn.

SATURDAY 1 ●

Moon in Capricorn.

SUNDAY 2 ●

Mercury trine Pluto; Venus sextile Neptune: romance, the arts and music may appeal. You may be forgetful or overly idealistic. Enjoy life, but avoid basing decisions on expectations alone. Travel or self-development may appeal. You may receive good news or news that means change. This is a good day to talk. Moon enters Aquarius.

| | | MAY | | | | |
S	M	T	W	T	F	S
						1
2	3	4	5	6	7	8
9	10	11	12	13	14	15
16	17	18	19	20	21	22
23	24	25	26	27	28	29
30	31					

MONDAY 3 ●

Sun square Saturn; Mercury square Jupiter: ensure you are super clear with communications to avoid mix-ups. You may need to accept your responsibilities and knuckle down at work. Moon in Aquarius.

TUESDAY 4 ◖

Moon in Aquarius.

WEDNESDAY 5 ◖

Moon in Pisces.

THURSDAY 6 ◖

Venus trine Pluto: this is a good day to make the changes you wish to see in your life, especially your personal life and financially. However, events may gain momentum, so ensure you're on track. Moon in Pisces.

FRIDAY 7 ☾

Moon enters Aries.

SATURDAY 8 ☾

Venus square Jupiter: you can accomplish a great deal, but you may experience a challenge. Be careful where you place your loyalties, as you may be easily led or your values may differ. Moon in Aries.

SUNDAY 9 ☾

Venus enters Gemini: you may feel more light-hearted or even ambivalent. If indecision arises, trust your values and principles regarding key matters over the coming weeks. Moon enters Taurus late at night.

| | | | MAY | | | |
S	M	T	W	T	F	S
						1
2	3	4	5	6	7	8
9	10	11	12	13	14	15
16	17	18	19	20	21	22
23	24	25	26	27	28	29
30	31					

MONDAY 10   (

Mercury conjunct moon's north node and Mercury semi-sextile Mars: a good day to talk and for meetings, but you must avoid rash decisions and hasty speech. Moon in Taurus.

TUESDAY 11   ○

New moon in Taurus; Mercury semi-sextile Uranus: travel plans, projects and conversations could go well but you must avoid impatience. You may feel the need for change in your life, but you must weigh your options carefully.

WEDNESDAY 12   )

Mercury trine Saturn; Mars sextile Uranus: you may feel ready for change and may be ready to embrace something new. Moon enters Gemini.

THURSDAY 13   )

Sun sextile Neptune; Jupiter enters Pisces: as Jupiter enters Pisces, you may initially feel disorientated but will soon gain ground. Art, music, romance, dance, film and spiritual development will soothe the soul. This may be a creative and romantic time, but you may also be easily misled. Moon in Gemini.

FRIDAY 14)

Moon in Gemini.

SATURDAY 15)

Mars quincunx Saturn: you'll appreciate the opportunity to get some chores done, even if you'd rather simply relax! Moon enters Cancer.

SUNDAY 16)

Moon in Cancer.

			MAY			
S	M	T	W	T	F	S
						1
2	3	4	5	6	7	8
9	10	11	12	13	14	15
16	17	18	19	20	21	22
23	24	25	26	27	28	29
30	31					

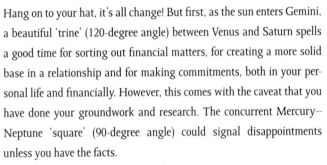

May to June 2021

Sun enters Gemini, May 20

Hang on to your hat, it's all change! But first, as the sun enters Gemini, a beautiful 'trine' (120-degree angle) between Venus and Saturn spells a good time for sorting out financial matters, for creating a more solid base in a relationship and for making commitments, both in your personal life and financially. However, this comes with the caveat that you have done your groundwork and research. The concurrent Mercury–Neptune 'square' (90-degree angle) could signal disappointments unless you have the facts.

Saturn will turn retrograde for nearly five months after May 23, which will provide the opportunity to reassess both your work circumstances and bigger picture goals. Take the opportunity to decide where your true duties rest, and ask yourself if you derive great pleasure from your work. If not, this is an excellent phase to reconsider your earning potential and work activities. Finalise key paperwork and decisions before May 23 to avoid delays. If you are undecided about how you wish to progress you will gain the opportunity to reconsider your situation, and details you learn will provide you with clarity by the end of June.

The sun in Gemini will certainly help with paperwork and communications, although once Mercury turns retrograde after May 29 you may find some aspects of communications, relationships and even travel become less smooth running.

The total lunar eclipse and supermoon on May 26 in Sagittarius will signal a fresh learning curve for all. You may be drawn to travel, adventure and study, or even to sort out legal matters. A matter of the heart may be a deciding factor in your decisions.

The annular solar eclipse on June 10 will be in Gemini and will again encourage a sense of new beginnings either in a relationship, in regard to a particular communication and, for some, at work.

You may experience a sense of destiny regarding new people you meet but must still exercise your usual discretion.

Developments mid-June, during the square between Saturn and Uranus, will let you know whether your situation and the changes you wish to make are viable. If not, it'll be back to the drawing board!

For Geminis

The upcoming eclipse season falls across your sign, signalling this month is a turning point for you either in a relationship (especially May-born Twins) or at work (especially June-born Twins). The first eclipse and supermoon on May 26 will be particularly powerful for those with birthdays then. Consider how to move ahead with your chosen decisions in the most practical and committed way.

For those Geminis experiencing changes in a key business or personal partnership, this is a time for well-informed and grounded decisions. Avoid being misled by expectations of an outcome; take your time to formulate the actions you must take. You may feel sentimental about some relationships but must be practical.

The extensive Saturn retrograde period until October will encourage you to work diligently towards an outcome. Mercury retrograde in Gemini from May 29 until June 22 likewise counsels research and diligence, both in your personal life and at work.

MONDAY 17 ☽

Sun trine Pluto: a good day to make changes where you feel these are necessary, even if you'd rather keep things as they are! Avoid excesses. Moon enters Leo.

TUESDAY 18 ☽

Venus semi-sextile Uranus: you'll enjoy doing something different. Someone may surprise you. Moon in Leo.

WEDNESDAY 19 ☽

Moon enters Virgo.

THURSDAY 20 ☽

Sun enters Gemini; Venus trine Saturn: a good time for making agreements and for making financial and personal commitments, as long as you have done your research where possible. Moon in Virgo.

FRIDAY 21

Sun square Jupiter: you can achieve a great deal but must be prepared to trust your instincts, especially if you come up against an obstacle to your plans. Be methodical. Moon in Virgo.

SATURDAY 22

Moon in Libra.

SUNDAY 23

Saturn turns retrograde; Mercury square Neptune: be inspired but be sure of the facts and figures before going head first into endeavours. Avoid delays and mix-ups by planning ahead. Moon in Libra.

		MAY				
S	M	T	W	T	F	S
						1
2	3	4	5	6	7	8
9	10	11	12	13	14	15
16	17	18	19	20	21	22
23	24	25	26	27	28	29
30	31					

MONDAY 24 ●

Venus semi-sextile Mars: this is a good day for talks but you must avoid rash decisions. Moon in Scorpio.

TUESDAY 25 ●

Moon in Scorpio.

WEDNESDAY 26 ●

Total lunar eclipse and supermoon in Sagittarius: be prepared to consider an adventure in a new light. You may be ready to leave a past circumstance behind but must be clear about your options.

THURSDAY 27 ●

Venus square Neptune: check your values: do they align with those of someone important, such as an employer or partner? Avoid making assumptions and over-indulgence. Gain the facts if making a key decision as mix-ups could arise. Moon in Sagittarius.

FRIDAY 28 ●

Moon in Capricorn.

SATURDAY 29 ●

Mercury turns retrograde; Mercury conjunct Venus: you may receive key news or take an important trip. A financial matter may deserve close attention. Moon in Capricorn.

SUNDAY 30 ●

Venus quincunx Pluto: ensure decisions align with your values. A challenge may arise, but you will overcome it with diligence. Moon enters Aquarius.

MAY

S	M	T	W	T	F	S
						1
2	3	4	5	6	7	8
9	10	11	12	13	14	15
16	17	18	19	20	21	22
23	24	25	26	27	28	29
30	31					

MONDAY 31

Sun conjunct moon's north node; Mars trine Neptune: you may meet someone you have a karmic connection with. You may be drawn to romance, art and music. Avoid making decisions without the facts. Moon in Aquarius.

TUESDAY 1

Moon in Pisces.

WEDNESDAY 2

Sun semi-sextile Uranus; Mercury semi-sextile Mars: this is a good day to review certain decisions and for a reunion. You may experience something new. Moon in Pisces.

THURSDAY 3

Sun trine Saturn; Venus trine Jupiter: this is a good day to work hard and to achieve your goals. It is also a good day to make commitments. You may be drawn to beauty, art, romance and love. Moon in Aries.

FRIDAY 4 ☾

Moon in Aries.

SATURDAY 5 ☾

Moon in Aries.

SUNDAY 6 ☾

Moon enters Taurus.

		JUNE				
S	M	T	W	T	F	S
		1	2	3	4	5
6	7	8	9	10	11	12
13	14	15	16	17	18	19
20	21	22	23	24	25	26
27	28	29	30			

JUNE

MONDAY 7   (

Moon in Taurus.

TUESDAY 8   (

Moon enters Gemini.

WEDNESDAY 9   (

Moon in Gemini.

THURSDAY 10   ○

*Annual solar eclipse in Gemini: the solar eclipse will be conjunct Mercury
and will signal key news, a meeting or developments that could alter your
circumstances considerably. Be open to the new, but ensure you research
circumstances carefully.*

FRIDAY 11)

Sun conjunct Mercury: key news, a meeting or a trip may be more significant than meets the eye, so be open to new opportunities but be prepared to look outside the box and check information. Moon in Cancer.

SATURDAY 12)

Moon in Cancer.

SUNDAY 13)

Sun square Neptune; Venus sextile Uranus: a surprise may arise. Someone may delight you with their news, but if the opposite occurs ensure you are practical and look for solutions. Moon enters Leo.

			JUNE			
S	M	T	W	T	F	S
		1	2	3	4	5
6	7	8	9	10	11	12
13	14	15	16	17	18	19
20	21	22	23	24	25	26
27	28	29	30			

MONDAY 14 ☽

Saturn square Uranus: this aspect points to a turning point in your year. Take note of bigger picture developments occurring around this time (not just today). Change cannot be avoided, so take the initiative. Moon in Leo.

TUESDAY 15 ☽

Moon in Leo.

WEDNESDAY 16 ☽

Mercury semi-sextile Venus: this is a good day to review your circumstances and for a reunion, and to discuss your options with those they concern. You may need to review a key financial matter. Moon enters Virgo.

THURSDAY 17 ☽

Sun quincunx Pluto: some changes may be more challenging than you imagine; stick at them and you will succeed. Moon in Virgo.

FRIDAY 18

Moon enters Libra.

SATURDAY 19

Moon in Libra.

SUNDAY 20

Moon enters Scorpio.

		JUNE				
S	M	T	W	T	F	S
		1	2	3	4	5
6	7	8	9	10	11	12
13	14	15	16	17	18	19
20	21	22	23	24	25	26
27	28	29	30			

June to July 2021

Sun enters Cancer, June 21

When the sun enters Cancer it marks the summer solstice in the northern hemisphere. The day is the longest, and we begin to consider the harvest time arriving soon. It is a time when our endeavours may peak and we realise the importance of self-nurture and nurturance of others.

The trine between the sun and Jupiter just after the solstice is a positive sign for growth in the areas of your life that are most important to you, and also for your own self-development. However, a little introspection and reliance on your gut feelings will be necessary, especially if you feel you are going over old ground and need direction moving forward.

The Capricorn full moon on June 24 will shine a light on your deeper emotions as simultaneously Venus will align opposite Pluto. You'll gain insight into areas where you wish to make considerable change. Take the next two weeks to formulate plans. You will do well to wait until the dust settles if emotions run high at this time.

Once Venus enters Leo on June 27 you may wish to include more romance, beauty and art in your everyday life and relationships over the next three weeks. Jupiter, Saturn, Pluto, Neptune and lastly Chiron will be retrograde this zodiacal month, so it will be in your interest to take your time with long-term decisions and to spend more time on the present and enjoying life.

A window of opportunity around the new moon on July 10 will help you put well-laid plans in motion, especially those that will affect your home life, property or spiritual understanding of your circumstances.

For Cancerians

With four planets retrograde from June 26 onwards, the next four weeks will be an ideal time to plan and strategise rather than to take action unless you already have plans in place at work, for example, that you must act upon. But for many Cancerians, this upcoming phase is more conducive to a little introspection and to re-orientate yourself.

Just after the sun enters Cancer a lovely event or activity will be inspiring, and this is a good time for holidays and to plan favourite activities you'll enjoy.

The Capricorn full moon on June 24 will spotlight changes at work and within your daily routine. If you feel you have outgrown your current schedule, the full moon will spotlight new interests and ideas. On the Cancerian new moon on July 10 you will be in a good position to put in place new plans to change areas of your life that you have outgrown.

The new moon will be an excellent time to reconsider elements of your personal life you'd like to change. A business or personal partnership may change footing, especially if it's your birthday around the new moon. If you're born later in July, prepare for a fresh daily or health routine to take root.

MONDAY 21 ●

Sun enters Cancer; Venus trine Neptune: the summer solstice. As the sun enters Cancer the summer solstice is a time to consider what you have achieved so far and the enjoyment of the harvest soon to come. Romance, the arts, beauty and self-improvement will all appeal. Moon in Scorpio.

TUESDAY 22 ●

Moon enters Sagittarius.

WEDNESDAY 23 ●

Sun trine Jupiter: you may feel optimistic; there may be upbeat news on the way. A trip should be enjoyable. Avoid excesses. Moon in Sagittarius.

THURSDAY 24 ●

Full moon in Capricorn; Venus opposite Pluto: strong emotions may arise. It's a good day to make changes, but you must ensure you have the full details and are not overly idealistic. Romance could flourish but so too could arguments.

FRIDAY 25 ●

Moon in Capricorn.

SATURDAY 26 ●

Moon enters Aquarius.

SUNDAY 27 ●

Venus enters Leo: you may wish to include more romance, beauty and art in your everyday life and relationships over the next three weeks. Moon in Aquarius.

		JUNE				
S	M	T	W	T	F	S
		1	2	3	4	5
6	7	8	9	10	11	12
13	14	15	16	17	18	19
20	21	22	23	24	25	26
27	28	29	30			

MONDAY 28

Moon enters Pisces.

TUESDAY 29

Venus quincunx Jupiter: step by step you will attain a goal, even if a hiccup arises. Moon in Pisces.

WEDNESDAY 30

Moon in Pisces.

THURSDAY 1

Mars opposite Saturn: this is a good day to get things done, but you must avoid impatience as it'll lead to frustration. You'll excel by being well organised. Moon in Aries.

FRIDAY 2 ◖

Moon in Aries.

SATURDAY 3 ◖

Sun quincunx Saturn: hard work will reap rewards; be diligent even if an obstacle arises. Moon enters Taurus.

SUNDAY 4 ◖

Mars square Uranus: you could go far, especially if you are patient and work hard, but impatience could trip you up. Be practical. Moon in Taurus.

			JULY			
S	M	T	W	T	F	S
				1	2	3
4	5	6	7	8	9	10
11	12	13	14	15	16	17
18	19	20	21	22	23	24
25	26	27	28	29	30	31

MONDAY 5 ⟨

Sun sextile Uranus: you may experience a pleasant surprise. If the opposite arises, see it as an opportunity to try something new. Moon in Taurus.

TUESDAY 6 ⟨

Mercury square Neptune: ensure you have the full details before jumping into projects, spending and investments head first. Avoid mix-ups by doing your research. Moon in Gemini.

WEDNESDAY 7 ⟨

Venus trine Chiron: you may experience a therapeutic development. You may be asked for help. Moon in Gemini.

THURSDAY 8 ⟨

Sun semi-sextile Mars; Venus square Uranus: be prepared to be adaptable but apply the brakes if you feel developments are counterproductive. If your values differ to someone else's, try to move ahead despite your differences. Moon enters Cancer.

FRIDAY 9

Moon in Cancer.

SATURDAY 10

New moon in Cancer: you may be ready for a fresh chapter; for some at home and for others in your emotional or spiritual life. Combine a nurturing approach with practicalities for the best results.

SUNDAY 11

Moon in Leo.

	JULY					
S	M	T	W	T	F	S
				1	2	3
4	5	6	7	8	9	10
11	12	13	14	15	16	17
18	19	20	21	22	23	24
25	26	27	28	29	30	31

MONDAY 12)

Mercury trine Jupiter: this is a good day for talks, get togethers and arranging travel. Moon in Leo.

TUESDAY 13)

Venus conjunct Mars: you may feel dynamic, making this a good day for get togethers, romance and adventure. A key financial transaction may take place. Moon enters Virgo.

WEDNESDAY 14)

Moon in Virgo.

THURSDAY 15)

Sun trine Neptune; Chiron turns retrograde: you'll enjoy the chance to indulge in your favourite activities but must avoid over-indulging and over-spending: you'll regret it! Moon enters Libra.

FRIDAY 16

Venus quincunx Neptune: you will attain your goals, even if you must work harder at them than usual. Art, romance and love will appeal. Moon in Libra.

SATURDAY 17

Sun opposite Pluto; Venus quincunx Pluto: you or someone close may have strong feelings. Tempers may flare. You could attain a goal. Romance could flourish. Moon enters Scorpio.

SUNDAY 18

Moon in Scorpio.

| | | JULY | | | | |
S	M	T	W	T	F	S
				1	2	3
4	5	6	7	8	9	10
11	12	13	14	15	16	17
18	19	20	21	22	23	24
25	26	27	28	29	30	31

July to August 2021

Sun enters Leo, July 22

Just after the sun enters Leo, four planets will change signs before the close of July. As they do, you will gain the opportunity to take action to make your projects work for you. You may be prone to change your mind about your circumstances now. Jupiter, Saturn and Pluto retrograde will all slow things down, so avoid taking impulsive action out of frustration with slow-moving circumstances.

Luckily, the Aquarian full moon on July 24 will add a sense of positive potential in the current climate, especially if you think outside the square. There is good news and/or the chance to deepen your appreciation of circumstances, and this will enable you to boost your circumstances long term.

Early August will be a good time to make a commitment or at least make a serious decision that could spell a more stable and secure phase for you to come during the rest of the year. What's more, the Leo new moon on August 8 will motivate you to put yourself centre stage and to make changes so that you are able to move ahead on a more solid platform.

Towards August 19 you are likely to experience developments that highlight the importance of being healthy in body, mind, spirit and emotions.

For Leos

In July, Mars in Leo opposite Jupiter may well bring your inner lion out, and your personal life will become the focus now. You may experience a particularly passionate time, which could translate as romance. But be aware that, as you fire up, you may experience opposition to your plans and arguments.

The Aquarian full moon on July 24 will draw intense energy from Pluto into the mix, once more adding to the picture of a potentially intense time due to changes to your daily routine and around how you will configure your work and health schedules so they work better with your ongoing circumstances. Consider how best to collaborate with those you work with, and how best to bring more compassion and understanding into your personal life.

The Leo new moon on August 8 will be an excellent time to reinvent yourself, and this may arise within your work, health or daily routine. And for Leos with birthdays around August 8 or before, a fresh commitment or fresh decision may be made in your personal life.

As Mercury conjuncts Mars towards August 19, you may experience an epiphany to do with finances or your personal life; ask yourself how you can improve these important areas. Simultaneously, a draw to your past, to someone who represents security and stability, will be hard to ignore.

MONDAY 19

Mercury square Chiron: avoid misunderstandings and traffic delays by planning ahead and being super clear. You may review a health matter. Moon enters Sagittarius.

TUESDAY 20

Mercury sextile Uranus: expect an unusual or out-of-the-ordinary event or news. This is a good day for meetings and a change of scenery. Moon in Sagittarius

WEDNESDAY 21

Moon enters Capricorn.

THURSDAY 22

Sun enters Leo; Venus enters Virgo; Venus opposite Jupiter: prepare to feel more expressive and to let your inner light shine. You may feel a little more creative; let your inner artist out. Moon in Capricorn.

FRIDAY 23 ●

Sun quincunx Jupiter: you may encounter a challenge, but it will encourage you to be stronger and more successful. Moon in Capricorn.

SATURDAY 24 ●

Full moon in Aquarius; Mercury trine Neptune: consider a fresh outlook. This is an excellent day to make changes to your health, looks and well-being. You may receive good news.

SUNDAY 25 ●

Mercury opposite Pluto: intense talks or a trip could signal a turning point. You may undergo a period of introspection. It is a good day to gain insight. Moon in Aquarius.

			JULY			
S	M	T	W	T	F	S
				1	2	3
4	5	6	7	8	9	10
11	12	13	14	15	16	17
18	19	20	21	22	23	24
25	26	27	28	29	30	31

MONDAY 26

Moon in Pisces.

TUESDAY 27

Mercury semi-sextile Mars: this is a good day to take the initiative, especially with written projects and key talks. Moon in Pisces.

WEDNESDAY 28

Jupiter enters Aquarius; Mercury quincunx Jupiter: you may gain the opportunity before the end of the year to make the changes you have been planning. The next five months are excellent to review your priorities. Moon enters Aries.

THURSDAY 29

Mars enters Virgo; Mars opposite Jupiter: you could make great progress but must avoid making snap decisions. You may review a past decision as you enter a phase of reflection and re-evaluation. Moon in Aries.

FRIDAY 30 ◖

Venus quincunx Saturn: a financial or personal matter may require you to rise to a challenge, but you have the ability to overcome it. Moon enters Taurus.

SATURDAY 31 ◖

Moon in Taurus.

SUNDAY 1 ◖

Sun conjunct Mercury; Mercury opposite Saturn: expect significant news or a trip. If news is not what you want it may nevertheless provide guidelines for moving forward. A father figure may have key news. Finances can be decided on. Moon in Taurus.

			AUGUST			
S	M	T	W	T	F	S
1	2	3	4	5	6	7
8	9	10	11	12	13	14
15	16	17	18	19	20	21
22	23	24	25	26	27	28
29	30	31				

MONDAY 2   ◖

Sun opposite Saturn: you may be ready to make a commitment. A financial decision may be made. Moon in Gemini.

TUESDAY 3   ◖

Venus trine Uranus: you may have an unexpected surprise. Moon in Gemini.

WEDNESDAY 4   ◖

Sun trine Chiron: this is a good day for a health and well-being treat. Someone may need your help or vice versa; rest assured help will be available. Moon enters Cancer.

THURSDAY 5   ◖

Mercury semi-sextile Venus: communications may flow better. It's a good day to raise key discussions. Financial matters may move quickly. Moon in Cancer.

FRIDAY 6   (

Sun square Uranus: expect an unexpected development. Think outside the square and be prepared to embrace or consider an out-of-the-ordinary solution to matters. Moon in Cancer.

SATUDAY 7   (

Moon enters Leo.

SUNDAY 8   ○

New moon in Leo; Mercury quincunx Neptune: time to turn a corner and put yourself centre stage. You may need to research information or be careful with conversations. Avoid misplacing objects.

		AUGUST				
S	M	T	W	T	F	S
1	2	3	4	5	6	7
8	9	10	11	12	13	14
15	16	17	18	19	20	21
22	23	24	25	26	27	28
29	30	31				

MONDAY 9)

Moon enters Virgo.

TUESDAY 10)

Venus opposite Neptune: art, music, creativity, film and dance will all appeal. It's a romantic day, so plan a treat! Avoid forgetfulness. Moon in Virgo.

WEDNESDAY 11)

Mercury enters Virgo; Mercury opposite Jupiter; Venus trine Pluto: key news or a trip will introduce new dynamics to your day. You may reconsider a decision or consider returning to an old haunt. You may wish to boost health. You could take great strides ahead today towards making long-term changes. Love and romance, meetings and creativity should be productive. Emotions may be particularly strong. Moon enters Libra.

THURSDAY 12)

Moon in Libra.

FRIDAY 13 ❭

Moon in Libra.

SATURDAY 14 ❭

Venus quincunx Jupiter: be careful with arrangements; avoid mix-ups. A plan may need to be rethought. You could make a breakthrough. Moon in Scorpio.

SUNDAY 15 ❭

Sun quincunx Neptune: pay attention to details or mistakes may be made. Moon in Scorpio.

			AUGUST			
S	M	T	W	T	F	S
1	2	3	4	5	6	7
8	9	10	11	12	13	14
15	16	17	18	19	20	21
22	23	24	25	26	27	28
29	30	31				

August to
september 2021

Sun enters Virgo August 22

Just before the sun enters Virgo, the sign known for being practical and perfectionistic, the moon will oppose it, making a full moon in the late degrees of Aquarius. Then, on September 20, there will be a Pisces full moon. This will be a quirky month despite the sun being in Virgo, and you may feel less well organised and practical than usual and a little more head in the clouds.

However, right-brain thinking, such as imagination, intuition, art and meditation, will thrive now; it will be a good time for gaining insight into how to be more aligned with your sense of purpose.

This zodiacal month is ideal for making resolutions for the remainder of the year, combining both your sense of practicalities and your imagination to create something in your life that is truly meaningful for yourself and your loved ones. But if you allow yourself to be easily distracted or easily led, you could end up somewhere you may not be happy about further down the line. A healthy balance between being committed to your plans and yet open to real and promising opportunity will ensure you stay on track.

The Virgo new moon on September 7 will be ideal for launching a fresh project or for taking the initiative to organise a revitalising health or work routine, even if the previous few days are littered with doubts or unreliable information. Aim to earth your projects and you could truly break new ground then.

For Virgos

The Aquarian full moon on August 22 will spotlight your imagination, spirituality and romantic life but also your resolve. You may feel particularly inspired at this time by someone special (particularly if it's your birthday), and a fresh interest in a work project may arise. The Pisces full moon on September 20 will once again bring your romantic, creative nature into being, prompting you to find ways to include more of the activities you love in your life.

The Virgo new moon on September 7 will help you to get your feet on the ground. It is an excellent time to turn a corner in your personal life, especially if you were born on that date or afterwards. Virgos born beforehand will find this month ideal for organising a fresh daily or work routine.

Health matters will also go well once you have all the information you need. The pitfall will be a lack of research and therefore a lack of information available to you.

Financially, once Venus enters Scorpio on September 10 you will gain a deeper appreciation of your circumstances.

If you feel disorientated this month, take time out and focus on your well-being.

MONDAY 16

Mercury quincunx Saturn: you could make great progress but you must plan ahead; be clear, compassionate and assertive if you face a challenge. Moon in Sagittarius.

TUESDAY 17

Sun quincunx Pluto: you could achieve a great deal but must avoid power struggles. Moon in Sagittarius.

WEDNESDAY 18

Mercury and Mars quincunx Chiron: if an obstacle arises you can overcome it with clever communication skills. Someone may ask for your help, or you may need someone's help yourself. Rest assured, it will be available. Moon in Capricorn.

THURSDAY 19

Mercury conjunct Mars: key news or developments are likely but you must avoid rushing ideas and projects. Avoid taking the random comments of other people personally. Moon in Capricorn.

FRIDAY 20 ●

Uranus begins a retrograde phase; Sun opposite Jupiter; Sun sesquiquadrate Chiron: you or someone close may make a mountain out of a molehill, so avoid exaggeration and grandstanding. You may experience considerable change such as a trip or a change of circumstance. It is a good day for a health appointment. Moon enters Aquarius.

SATURDAY 21 ●

Moon in Aquarius.

SUNDAY 22 ●

Full moon in Aquarius; sun enters Virgo; Mars trine Uranus: time to focus on health, well-being, work and being helpful over the next few weeks. This may be a varied day and you may experience a surprise, a light-bulb moment or an out-of-the-ordinary circumstance. Sun enters Pisces in the afternoon.

			AUGUST			
S	M	T	W	T	F	S
1	2	3	4	5	6	7
8	9	10	11	12	13	14
15	16	17	18	19	20	21
22	23	24	25	26	27	28
29	30	31				

MONDAY 23 ●

Venus trine Saturn: a good day to be practical, especially with finances and planning. Romance could flourish; a commitment may be made. Moon in Pisces.

TUESDAY 24 ●

Moon enters Aries.

WEDNESDAY 25 ●

Mercury opposite Neptune: a trip or meeting could be ideal but you must avoid delays, absentmindedness and misunderstandings. Romance and enjoyable ventures will appeal. Moon in Aries.

THURSDAY 26 ●

Moon in Aries.

FRIDAY 27

Mercury quincunx Jupiter: you will rise to the challenge to overcome an obstacle such as a difficult communication or travel delay. Moon in Taurus.

SATURDAY 28

Venus quincunx Uranus: you may experience a surprise this weekend. If you must undergo a complex development, rest assured you will overcome it. Moon in Taurus.

SUNDAY 29

Moon enters Gemini.

		AUGUST				
S	M	T	W	T	F	S
1	2	3	4	5	6	7
8	9	10	11	12	13	14
15	16	17	18	19	20	21
22	23	24	25	26	27	28
29	30	31				

MONDAY 30 ◖

Moon in Gemini.

TUESDAY 31 ◖

Sun quincunx Saturn: approach an authority figure tactfully and be aware of rules and regulations; hard work will reap rewards. Moon in Gemini.

WEDNESDAY 1 ◖

Moon enters Cancer.

THURSDAY 2 ◖

Mars opposite Neptune: well-laid plans should go well, but you must avoid heated discussions, impulsiveness, forgetfulness and idealism. The arts, romance and music will appeal. It is a good day for meditation. Moon in Cancer.

FRIDAY 3 (

Moon enters Leo.

SATURDAY 4 (

Venus quincunx Neptune: you'll overcome obstacles but must avoid idealism when negotiating with unreliable or tricky people. Moon in Leo.

SUNDAY 5 (

Mercury trine Saturn: this is a good day for talks with authority figures and for making a commitment. You may need to draw on your resources to find a way around an obstacle. Moon in Leo.

		SEPTEMBER				
S	M	T	W	T	F	S
			1	2	3	4
5	6	7	8	9	10	11
12	13	14	15	16	17	18
19	20	21	22	23	24	25
26	27	28	29	30		

MONDAY 6 (

Mars trine Pluto; Venus trine Jupiter: you may feel particularly motivated to get things done. Avoid being impatient; be well organised instead. Romance and love could blossom. Moon enters Virgo.

TUESDAY 7 ○

New moon in Virgo; sun trine Uranus: a good time to launch a work project or venture as long as you have the full facts and have done your groundwork. You may experience a considerable surprise or coincidence today.

WEDNESDAY 8)

Mercury opposite Chiron: you may receive key news or undergo a significant trip. It is a good day for a medical or beauty appointment. You may be asked to help someone or must ask for support yourself. Moon enters Libra.

THURSDAY 9)

Moon in Libra.

FRIDAY 10 ❯

Venus enters Scorpio; Mercury quincunx Uranus: you may experience unusual developments or will need to change your usual schedule. You may feel like kicking up your heels. Moon enters Scorpio.

SATURDAY 11 ❯

Jupiter semi-sextile Pluto: a trip, meeting or chat may have a transformational effect. Moon in Scorpio.

SUNDAY 12 ❯

Moon enters Sagittarius.

			SEPTEMBER			
S	M	T	W	T	F	S
			1	2	3	4
5	6	7	8	9	10	11
12	13	14	15	16	17	18
19	20	21	22	23	24	25
26	27	28	29	30		

MONDAY 13

Moon in Sagittarius.

TUESDAY 14

Sun opposite Neptune: you'll be inspired by nature, art and your imagination. You may feel super creative, romantic and idealistic. You may need to focus hard at work or risk being easily distracted. Moon enters Capricorn.

WEDNESDAY 15

Mars enters Libra: you will feel motivated to gain more balance and harmony in your life over the coming weeks but at first may experience a sense of disorder or discord. Be practical and look for solutions. Moon in Capricorn.

THURSDAY 16

Sun quincunx Jupiter: if you encounter a hurdle, rest assured you will overcome it with a clever mix of innovation and method. Moon enters Aquarius.

FRIDAY 17 ●

Sun trine Pluto; Venus square Saturn: a good day to make changes where you feel they're necessary, even if you'd rather keep things as they are! Be practical and look outside the square. Avoid impulsiveness and obstinacy. Moon in Aquarius.

SATURDAY 18 ●

Mercury quincunx Neptune: you may need to research information or be careful with communications, travel and information. Avoid misplacing objects. Moon enters Pisces.

SUNDAY 19 ●

Moon in Pisces.

		SEPTEMBER				
S	M	T	W	T	F	S
			1	2	3	4
5	6	7	8	9	10	11
12	13	14	15	16	17	18
19	20	21	22	23	24	25
26	27	28	29	30		

september to october 2021

Sun enters Libra, September 22

As the sun enters Libra this is the autumn equinox. And, as the seasons change, this is a good time to seek more harmony and balance in your home life as you may be spending more time indoors.

If developments around September 23 seem anything but peaceful and balanced, ensure you take action to avoid them snowballing. You will gain an idea of the areas of your life that will require additional focus at this time.

Once Mercury turns retrograde after September 27, you may find communications take a difficult turn until at least October 17. Mercury's particular position on September 27 spells complications. You may need to review or to revisit decisions or matters that arose in August and earlier in September during this retrograde phase.

The positive alignments early in October between the sun, Mars, Mercury and Saturn are ideal both for goal setting and goal getting. However, if you find that matters that are out of your control snowball, it'll be important now to make decisions with a long-term view as your actions will have long-term consequences.

The Aries full moon on October 20 will once again show you just where you need more balance in life, so be prepared then to adjust your plans to suit prevailing circumstances and take positive action.

For Librans

The sun and Mars in Libra make a positive aspect with Saturn and then with Jupiter, offering optimum circumstances to build a sense of togetherness at home. If you work from home or with property you are likely to make a great deal of progress at work.

If your partner or those you work with can be unpredictable watch out, especially around September 23, as they may behave true to form! If their input in your life is generally upbeat it will probably continue to be so, but if it can be disruptive then prepare to work around their erratic mindsets.

Singles may bump into someone unexpectedly who opens your eyes to a new kind of relationship.

A financial matter will deserve careful scrutiny. Once Mercury turns retrograde after September 27, you will gain the opportunity to review your budget and put a more secure one in place.

The Libran new moon on October 6 will offer the chance to re-invent yourself, and doing something different may appeal to you, be this with your appearance, health-wise or at work. The chance for an adventure is likely throughout October, as new horizons beckon.

A relationship will be a focus at the Aries full moon on October 20; be prepared to adjust to circumstances then that may develop rapidly.

MONDAY 20 ●

Full moon in Pisces; Mercury trine Jupiter: romance is alive! You may be a little head in the clouds and may even feel a little disorganised, so ensure you focus at work or mistakes may be made. A trip may be pivotal. Plan ahead to avoid travel delays.

TUESDAY 21 ●

Moon in Aries.

WEDNESDAY 22 ●

Sun enters Libra; Mercury square Pluto; autumn equinox: a time to integrate ideas, give thanks and prepare for winter. Look for balance and a fair go over the coming weeks. Avoid arguments and delays by planning ahead and being patient. Moon in Aries.

THURSDAY 23 ●

Venus opposite Uranus: expect an unexpected development; someone may behave erratically or will surprise you. Moon enters Taurus.

FRIDAY 24 ●

Moon in Taurus.

SATURDAY 25 ●

Mars trine Saturn: this trine could catapult your projects into new territory, especially if you are well prepared, but if you have ventures you are unclear about you may find events take a momentum of their own. Be well prepared but also be open to new ideas. Moon in Taurus.

SUNDAY 26 ●

Moon in Gemini.

		SEPTEMBER				
S	M	T	W	T	F	S
			1	2	3	4
5	6	7	8	9	10	11
12	13	14	15	16	17	18
19	20	21	22	23	24	25
26	27	28	29	30		

MONDAY 27

Mercury turns retrograde: you may receive news that merits careful thought. Moon in Gemini.

TUESDAY 28

Moon enters Cancer.

WEDNESDAY 29

Sun trine Saturn; Venus trine Neptune: today could be ideal for reigniting passion and romance in your life. However, you may be easily misled, so focus on priorities and this could be a successful time. Moon in Cancer.

THURSDAY 30

Moon in Cancer.

LIBRA

FRIDAY 1 ◖

Mercury square Pluto; Mars opposite Chiron: this is a good day to focus on well-being and health. Avoid taking someone's random comments personally. An issue stemming back a week may resurface or will require focus. Avoid rash decisions. Moon in Leo.

SATURDAY 2 ◖

Venus sextile Pluto: a good day to make changes you've researched. You'll enjoy a get together. Moon in Leo.

SUNDAY 3 ◖

Mercury trine Jupiter: a trip or events may remind you of developments at the last full moon. Moon enters Virgo.

OCTOBER

S	M	T	W	T	F	S
					1	2
3	4	5	6	7	8	9
10	11	12	13	14	15	16
17	18	19	20	21	22	23
24	25	26	27	28	39	30
31						

MONDAY 4   (

Moon in Virgo.

TUESDAY 5   (

Mercury quincunx Neptune: you may need to research information or be careful with conversations, travel and information. Avoid misplacing objects. Moon enters Libra.

WEDNESDAY 6   ○

New moon in Libra; Mars quincunx Uranus: a chance to establish more balance and harmony in your life may arise from out of the blue, and you may also gain the opportunity to boost your skillset. You'll find answers to problems but must avoid impulsiveness.

THURSDAY 7   )

Venus enters Sagittarius; sun quincunx Uranus: an unexpected change of plan or a surprise may arise. Someone may behave unpredictably. Adventure such as long-distance travel may appeal. Moon enters Scorpio.

FRIDAY 8)

Sun conjunct Mars: events could snowball or occur without notice. Avoid anger and impatience; these will be pitfalls. Moon in Scorpio.

SATURDAY 9)

Sun conjunct Mercury; Mercury conjunct Mars: communications may be busy; you may receive key news or a guest or undergo a trip – or all three! Be spontaneous but avoid snap decisions; they may trip you up. Moon in Sagittarius.

SUNDAY 10)

Moon in Sagittarius.

		OCTOBER				
S	M	T	W	T	F	S
					1	2
3	4	5	6	7	8	9
10	11	12	13	14	15	16
17	18	19	20	21	22	23
24	25	26	27	28	39	30
31						

MONDAY 11 ☽

Moon enters Capricorn.

TUESDAY 12 ☽

Mercury quincunx Uranus: restlessness may contribute to impulsiveness. You may hear unexpectedly about a change of plan. Moon in Capricorn.

WEDNESDAY 13 ☽

Venus sextile Saturn: this is a good day to make serious decisions and for work meetings and to make a commitment. Think outside the square for the best results. Moon enters Aquarius.

THURSDAY 14 ☽

Moon in Aquarius.

FRIDAY 15 ●

Sun trine Jupiter: a good day to get in touch with like-minded people and to enjoy fun and something different. Moon in Aquarius.

SATURDAY 16 ●

Venus trine Chiron: this is a good day for health and beauty treats, but you must be clear about what you want. A therapeutic or healing atmosphere will appeal. Moon in Pisces.

SUNDAY 17 ●

Mercury ends its retrograde phase; sun square Pluto; Mercury sextile Venus; Mars quincunx Neptune: an excellent day to get in touch with someone you love and to spend time on your favourite endeavours, but you must avoid making assumptions or arguments could arise and your vulnerabilities peak. Moon in Pisces.

			OCTOBER			
S	M	T	W	T	F	S
					1	2
3	4	5	6	7	8	9
10	11	12	13	14	15	16
17	18	19	20	21	22	23
24	25	26	27	28	39	30
31						

october to november 2021

Sun enters Scorpio, October 23

As the sun enters passionate Scorpio, the concurrent Mars square Pluto will add to the feeling of intensity this Scorpio month. If you have already been experiencing tension, make plans to deactivate some of the negative trends in your life or sparks will fly! One thing is certain: passions will ramp up over the coming weeks, especially once war-like Mars enters Scorpio on October 30, where it will be until mid-December.

You won't be the only one with a stubborn and war-like attitude, so if you prefer peace find ways to navigate through this intense time or arguments and opposition will characterise this Scorpio month.

The Scorpio new moon supermoon on November 4 will be a fiery one and at the least will include a surprise. It will be a good time to launch a new project or to begin a fresh relationship if you like ventures to develop quickly. However, arguments may be rife and relationships volatile, so consider finding ways to inject more peace in relationships and work towards a sense of conciliation if life becomes drama fuelled.

If you feel certain parameters at work or in your personal life no longer resonate with you on a purposeful level, this will be a month when changes can be made. You may even be surprised by the suddenness with which some changes take place.

For Scorpios

The Scorpio new moon supermoon on November 4 will offer a great opportunity to change dynamics in a work or personal context. If you avoid stubbornness, a new and progressive agreement can be put in place. You may seek to change the parameters of some of your agreements and, if some relationships have run their course, it will be time to take a fresh path.

Watch out, though: this is a high-energy month, when tempers and tantrums could take hold and plans you have not thought through adequately could cause disruptions.

Once Mercury joins Mars in your sign on November 5 you are likely to throw caution to the wind, and will enjoy indulging in all the delights life has to offer. This will be an ideal time for creative work and your love life, but it could wreak havoc with your work life and even family relationships as your intense and fun-loving side will seek expression.

The Taurean partial lunar eclipse on November 19 will once again highlight your business or personal partnerships. If you didn't make considerable changes either at work or in a personal relationship earlier in November, this eclipse will spotlight where changes must be made now.

MONDAY 18 ●

Moon enters Aries.

TUESDAY 19 ●

Venus quincunx Uranus: an unexpected development needn't throw a spanner in the works; it could open new doors. If a hurdle arises, rest assured you will overcome it. Moon in Aries.

WEDNESDAY 20 ●

Full moon in Aries: this will be a powerful full moon as it aligns opposite fiery Mars. Expect developments to move quickly at the least. It is a good time to seek peace and harmony; your plans could gain traction. Moon enters Taurus at night.

THURSDAY 21 ●

Moon in Taurus.

FRIDAY 22 ●

Mars square Pluto: you could achieve a great deal now with determination and application but must avoid a battle of egos, as it could spiral into conflict. Moon in Taurus.

SATURDAY 23 ●

Sun enters Scorpio: passion will ramp up over the coming weeks! Moon enters Gemini.

SUNDAY 24 ●

Mercury quincunx Uranus: you will gain the chance to overcome a misunderstanding or difficult communication. Plan ahead to avoid travel delays. Moon in Gemini.

OCTOBER

S	M	T	W	T	F	S
					1	2
3	4	5	6	7	8	9
10	11	12	13	14	15	16
17	18	19	20	21	22	23
24	25	26	27	28	39	30
31						

MONDAY 25

Moon enters Cancer.

TUESDAY 26

Moon in Cancer.

WEDNESDAY 27

Venus square Neptune: check your values: do they align with those of someone important? Avoid making assumptions and impulsiveness. Gain the facts if making a key decision. Be prepared to check details, as mix-ups could occur. Moon in Cancer.

THURSDAY 28

Venus sextile Jupiter: you'll enjoy getting together with an adventurous, upbeat character. Consider exciting plans in more detail; they could be viable. Moon enters Leo.

FRIDAY 29   ☾

Moon in Leo.

SATURDAY 30   ☾

Mars enters Scorpio; sun square Saturn; Venus semi-sextile Pluto: a particular responsibility may require more focus. Someone in control of some of your circumstances may exercise their authority. You'll enjoy a lovely get together but must avoid misunderstandings. If you're travelling, plan ahead to avoid delays. Moon enters Virgo.

SUNDAY 31   ☾

Happy Hallowe'en! Moon in Virgo.

		OCTOBER				
S	M	T	W	T	F	S
					1	2
3	4	5	6	7	8	9
10	11	12	13	14	15	16
17	18	19	20	21	22	23
24	25	26	27	28	39	30
31						

MONDAY 1   (

Mercury trine Jupiter: communications will progress under their own steam. A trip should be enjoyable but may include an element of surprise. Moon enters Libra.

TUESDAY 2   (

Mercury square Pluto: you may be challenged to excel; an important meeting or communication will merit careful thought. Avoid arguments, as they may escalate quickly. Moon in Libra.

WEDNESDAY 3   (

Moon in Libra.

THURSDAY 4   ○

New moon supermoon in Scorpio opposite Uranus: the new moon may carry a surprise, so be prepared to embrace something new. An unexpected development such as news from an old friend or bumping into someone will arise. News may open doors.

FRIDAY 5 ⟩

Mercury enters Scorpio: communications are likely to become more in-depth, intense or even probing over the coming weeks. Watch out: a secret may be revealed! Moon in Scorpio.

SATURDAY 6 ⟩

Mercury sextile Venus: a good day for talks and meetings. A financial matter could progress. Moon in Sagittarius.

SUNDAY 7 ⟩

Moon in Sagittarius.

		NOVEMBER				
S	M	T	W	T	F	S
	1	2	3	4	5	6
7	8	9	10	11	12	13
14	15	16	17	18	19	20
21	22	23	24	25	26	27
28	29	30				

MONDAY 8   )

Moon in Capricorn.

TUESDAY 9   )

Moon in Capricorn.

WEDNESDAY 10   )

Mercury conjunct Mars; Mercury and Mars square Saturn: communications are likely to be busy or complicated. Avoid impulsiveness, or you may reveal more than you wish to. You may enjoy a spontaneous get together. Moon in Aquarius.

THURSDAY 11   )

Moon in Aquarius.

FRIDAY 12

Sun trine Neptune: romance will motivate you; you'll be inspired by the arts and music; someone may be particularly persuasive. Avoid forgetfulness. Moon enters Pisces.

SATURDAY 13

Mercury opposite Uranus: you may hear unexpected news or will enjoy a spontaneous event. Avoid snap decisions; think things through. Moon in Pisces.

SUNDAY 14

Venus semi-sextile Saturn: a good day to make a commitment to a plan of action, especially regarding love and finances. Moon enters Aries.

NOVEMBER

S	M	T	W	T	F	S
	1	2	3	4	5	6
7	8	9	10	11	12	13
14	15	16	17	18	19	20
21	22	23	24	25	26	27
28	29	30				

MONDAY 15 ●

Sun square Jupiter: you can achieve a great deal but must be prepared to trust your instincts, especially if you come up against an obstacle to your plans. Be inspired but avoid snap decisions. Moon in Aries.

TUESDAY 16 ●

Sun sextile Pluto: a good day to make changes in your life, but you must avoid impulsiveness. Moon in Aries.

WEDNESDAY 17 ●

Mars opposite Uranus: developments may occur rapidly. You may experience a surprise or unexpected circumstance. Moon in Taurus.

THURSDAY 18 ●

Mercury trine Neptune: you'll feel inspired by someone or by the arts, movies or dance. You may feel particularly romantic or talkative. Moon in Taurus.

FRIDAY 19 ●

Partial lunar eclipse in Taurus; Venus trine Uranus: expect change! And it's likely to surround money, love or your feelings. Moon enters Gemini in the afternoon.

SATURDAY 20 ●

Mercury square Jupiter: words will flow, so choose them carefully. Plan travel ahead to avoid delays. Set clever plans in motion but be adaptable. Moon in Gemini.

SUNDAY 21 ●

Mercury sextile Pluto: make changes in areas of your life where you know it is needed the most. Communications should go well, but you must be flexible and willing to collaborate. Moon in Gemini.

NOVEMBER

S	M	T	W	T	F	S
	1	2	3	4	5	6
7	8	9	10	11	12	13
14	15	16	17	18	19	20
21	22	23	24	25	26	27
28	29	30				

November to December 2021

Sun enters Sagittarius, November 22

The sun and Mercury in Sagittarius will add to a more upbeat, outgoing and adventurous atmosphere. The end of November has particularly positive astrological aspects that could truly help you get ahead with your various plans, so ensure you take the initiative and power ahead.

However, this is an eclipse season, and the solar eclipse in Sagittarius on December 4 will highlight the importance of getting communications, travel and your long-term plans straight, such as plans that involve general broadening of your horizons including study or legal matters.

This eclipse season may highlight which areas of your life are progressing well and which seem stuck. The upside is that you will gain clarity about the areas that need a little push in the right direction so you can progress.

December 4 to 7 may involve the need to rethink some plans, or simply to be more diligent with those you already have in place.

Once Mercury has entered Capricorn and Mars has entered Sagittarius after December 13, you may gain the opportunity to feel more settled in your ventures and in your mind.

The Gemini full moon on December 19 will once again put the focus firmly on the importance of good communication skills – and also on the importance of fun – just in time for holidays and Christmas! The conjunction of Venus with Pluto will merit a sense of both good humor and good communication skills to ensure you navigate a potentially intense time skilfully.

For Sagittarians

Mars in Scorpio and then in your own sign spells a sociable time, and you will enjoy meeting new people and indulging in your favorite activities.

The conjunction of the sun and Mercury in your sign at the end of November signals key news, and the chance to kick start a fresh, healing cycle in your life. For some healing will occur principally in connection with a key relationship, while for others it will be via work or due to a new health routine.

The Sagittarian solar eclipse on December 4 will again highlight the beginning of a fresh phase in your life (especially if it's your birthday then), and all Sagittarians will experience a revitalising new chapter. However, to move into a fresh circumstance you will need to let go of old habits and to embrace new ones. Luckily, being an adventurous character, making changes is easier than it is for many other signs. Financial arrangements may be particularly in need of focus this month, especially around December 10-11.

The Gemini full moon on December 19 will spotlight a business or personal partnership. You may take a fresh path with certain relationships or arrangements that have been at breaking point for some time. Singles who have been single for a while may meet someone who could become a special companion and partner.

MONDAY 22

Sun enters Sagittarius: let your inner adventurer out over the coming weeks. Moon enters Cancer.

TUESDAY 23

Moon in Cancer.

WEDNESDAY 24

Mercury enters Sagittarius: communications, socialising and the potential for travel will become more upbeat and viable over the next two and a half weeks. Moon enters Leo.

THURSDAY 25

Moon in Leo.

FRIDAY 26   ◗

Moon in Leo.

SATURDAY 27   ◗

Jupiter semi-sextile Pluto; Saturn sextile Chiron: a good day to make the changes that are needed in your life. Be methodical and work out new ways to get things done. Moon in Virgo.

SUNDAY 28   ◗

Moon in Virgo.

			NOVEMBER			
S	M	T	W	T	F	S
	1	2	3	4	5	6
7	8	9	10	11	12	13
14	15	16	17	18	19	20
21	22	23	24	25	26	27
28	29	30				

MONDAY 29 (

Sun conjunct Mercury; Mars trine Neptune: a lovely day for a get together. You may receive key news. You'll appreciate the chance to indulge in a favourite activity. Follow your instincts if you're unsure of a decision. Moon enters Libra.

TUESDAY 30 (

Sun and Mercury trine Chiron; Mercury sextile Saturn; Venus sextile Neptune: a good time to research your circumstances, especially financially. You may receive good news or will find out better where you stand with someone. A good day for a health or beauty appointment. Romance could blossom. Moon in Libra.

WEDNESDAY 1 (

Moon enters Scorpio.

THURSDAY 2 (

Mercury quincunx Uranus: you may hear unexpected news. Plan ahead to avoid travel delays. Moon in Scorpio.

FRIDAY 3 (

Moon enters Sagittarius.

SATURDAY 4 ○

Total solar eclipse in Sagittarius: prepare for a fresh phase, which may involve an adventurous or exciting project, travel or simply the need to broaden your horizons.

SUNDAY 5)

Moon enters Capricorn.

		DECEMBER				
S	M	T	W	T	F	S
			1	2	3	4
5	6	7	8	9	10	11
12	13	14	15	16	17	18
19	20	21	22	23	24	25
26	27	28	29	30	31	

MONDAY 6)

Mars sextile Pluto: a good day to set key plans in motion. Events may snowball, so be prepared to apply the brakes if things speed up too fast. Moon in Capricorn.

TUESDAY 7)

Mercury square Neptune: ensure you have all the information you need, as otherwise mistakes could be made. Plan travel ahead to avoid delays. Moon enters Aquarius.

WEDNESDAY 8)

Mars square Jupiter: if you encounter an obstacle, avoid being impulsive; patience will work far better. You could achieve a goal. Moon in Aquarius.

THURSDAY 9)

Moon enters Pisces.

FRIDAY 10 ❯

Mercury semi-sextile Venus and Pluto: a good day to talk, and for get togethers and romance. A change of environment could appeal. Moon in Pisces.

SATURDAY 11 ▶

Mercury sextile Jupiter; Venus conjunct Pluto: an intense but enjoyable day is likely. If you find today's events lacking in enjoyment, take time out to gather your thoughts. Someone may need your help. A financial commitment may be made. Romance and the arts could flourish. Moon enters Aries.

SUNDAY 12 ▶

Sun square Neptune: ensure you research circumstances if making key decisions. Avoid forgetfulness; keep an eye on house keys, for example. Moon in Aries.

| | | DECEMBER | | | | |
S	M	T	W	T	F	S
			1	2	3	4
5	6	7	8	9	10	11
12	13	14	15	16	17	18
19	20	21	22	23	24	25
26	27	28	29	30	31	

MONDAY 13

Mercury enters Capricorn; Mars enters Sagittarius; Mercury semi-sextile Mars: a change of mood may draw on your inner resources. Luckily, communications should be clear but may gather momentum, so this could be a busy day. Moon in Aries.

TUESDAY 14

Moon enters Taurus.

WEDNESDAY 15

Moon in Taurus.

THURSDAY 16

Moon enters Gemini.

FRIDAY 17 ●

Sun semi-sextile Pluto: a good day to make changes, especially involving love, money and self-empowerment. Moon in Gemini.

SATURDAY 18 ●

Sun semi-sextile Venus: you'll appreciate the opportunity to enjoy the company of like-minded people or someone you love. You may enjoy a beauty or health boost. Romance could blossom but you must avoid misunderstandings. Moon in Gemini.

SUNDAY 19 ●

Full moon in Gemini; Mercury square Chiron: the spotlight will be on fun, communications and, for some, travel. You'll enjoy doing something different. Check travel plans to avoid delays and misunderstandings. Moon enters Cancer later in the day.

			DECEMBER			
S	M	T	W	T	F	S
			1	2	3	4
5	6	7	8	9	10	11
12	13	14	15	16	17	18
19	20	21	22	23	24	25
26	27	28	29	30	31	

December 2021

Sun enters Capricorn, December 21

As the sun steps into Capricorn, this marks the winter solstice in the northern hemisphere, a time when we collectively reflect on the hard work we have done all year and prepare to plant new seeds of hope for the coming year.

This year's Capricorn season will be particularly poignant as it will feature the square between Saturn and Uranus on Christmas Eve, an aspect that will characterise 2022. This square is an echo of the opposition between the two planets that occurred in 2008, when the structure and function in your life may have altered considerably. Now we are once again at the brink of beginning a fresh arrangement in our lives, and this month's developments will provide a heads up for the type of developments to come in 2022.

But back to December: just as the sun steps into practical Capricorn, the mood moves increasingly to the practical and to planning: just in time for Christmas and the start of 2022. The conjunction of Venus with Pluto on Christmas Day could lead to fireworks, so if you do not like drama keep your head focused on harmony and let the only loud noise be the bon bons at the dinner table!

Focus on refuelling energy levels in the last week of December as 2022 promises to be another year of restructuring, one where planning will be a true forte.

For more about Capricorn in January 2022, reserve your copy of the *2022 Astrology Diary*; see Rockpool Publishing at www.rockpoolpublishing.co and www.patsybennett.com.

Wishing everyone a very happy solstice, Yuletide and a happy New Year!

For Capricorns

Just as the sun enters your sign, the conjunction of Venus and Pluto spells an intense few days. If you prefer life to be on an even keel, plan ahead to avoid fireworks. And, if 2021 has already been a drama-fuelled year, aim to keep the lid on high emotions and set your intention to break into a new mould in 2022. It will be possible; start planning now! You will gain insight in the last 10 days of 2021 into the kinds of structures in your life that will merit an overhaul. For many, these will involve your personal, family life and/or finances; for some, work and home life too. Be prepared to step into the new in 2022, because nothing holds change back when Saturn and Uranus engage each other.

The concomitant Neptune-Pluto sextile spells the chance for a beautiful change in your environment that may come about through love or romance. Bear in mind this could spell peace and harmony – but it may also be a sign of overt idealism. As always, keep your feet on the ground and reach for the stars.

MONDAY 20 ●

Sun sextile Jupiter; Mercury trine Uranus; Venus turns retrograde; Chiron ends a five-month retrograde phase: an optimistic frame of mind will accomplish great feats. This may be an intense time. Aim to defuse tension. Romance could blossom. Moon in Cancer.

TUESDAY 21 ●

Sun enters Capricorn: as, collectively, thoughts turn to the practicalities of the holiday season and 2022, today's serendipitous vibe will raise moods. Moon enters Leo.

WEDNESDAY 22 ●

Moon in Leo.

THURSDAY 23 ●

Moon in Leo.

FRIDAY 24

Saturn square Uranus: an unexpected development needn't throw a spanner in the works. You'll find practical ways to overcome any obstacles. Moon enters Virgo.

SATURDAY 25

Venus conjunct Pluto: Merry Christmas! Focus on practicalities for a fun time. Intense feelings may emerge that may take you back into the past. Avoid drama by focusing on positives. Moon in Virgo.

SUNDAY 26

Mercury sextile Neptune: a more relaxed day is likely, and you'll enjoy get togethers. Avoid over-indulging and over-spending at the sales; you may regret it! Moon enters Libra.

		DECEMBER				
S	M	T	W	T	F	S
			1	2	3	4
5	6	7	8	9	10	11
12	13	14	15	16	17	18
19	20	21	22	23	24	25
26	27	28	29	30	31	

MONDAY 27   ☾

Moon in Libra.

TUESDAY 28   ☾

Moon enters Scorpio.

WEDNESDAY 29   ☾

Sun square Chiron; Mercury conjunct Venus; Mars quincunx Uranus: you may experience a surprise or a delay. A key trip or meeting will arise. Moon in Scorpio.

THURSDAY 30   ☾

Mercury conjunct Pluto; Mars sextile Saturn: you may feel adventurous over the next two days and you'll enjoy a get together. An agreement can be made, but you must avoid snap decisions and drama. Moon enters Sagittarius.

FRIDAY 31   (

Happy New Year! Moon in Sagittarius.

SATURDAY 1

SUNDAY 2

			DECEMBER			
S	M	T	W	T	F	S
			1	2	3	4
5	6	7	8	9	10	11
12	13	14	15	16	17	18
19	20	21	22	23	24	25
26	27	28	29	30	31	

NOTES

NOTES

NOTES

NOTES

NOTES

About the author

Patsy Bennett is a rare combination of astrologer and psychic medium. Her horoscopes are published in over 65 newspapers and magazines throughout Australia and internationally, including *The New Zealand TV Guide* and *The Sunshine Coast Daily*. Her articles have been published in newspapers and magazines, including *Take 5* and *Practical Parenting*. Patsy has appeared on several live daytime TV and radio shows, including *Studio 10* and *The Project*. Her first astrology book, *Astrology: Secrets of the Moon*, was published in October 2015, and her *Astrology Diaries* and *Zodiac Moon Reading Cards* are also published by Rockpool Publishing.

Born in New Zealand, Patsy relocated to the UK where, in the 1980s, she worked as a sub-editor and production editor for women's and fashion magazines, including *Woman's Own* and *ELLE* (UK). She studied astrology at the Faculty of Astrological Studies in London in the 1990s then in 1998 relocated to Australia, where she worked as a reporter for local newspapers in the northern New South Wales area while continuing her practice as an astrologer.

Patsy has worked as a professional astrologer for over 23 years. She began reading palms and tarot at age 14, and experienced mediumistic insights as young as age 12. She is a natural medium and has perfected her skill by studying with some of the world's foremost mediums. Patsy provides astrology and psychic intuitive consultations and facilitates astrology and psychic development workshops in northern New South Wales and on the Gold Coast in Queensland.

Patsy gained a Master of Arts degree in Romance Languages and Literature at the University of London and taught French at the University of California, Berkeley. She is a member of the Queensland Federation of Astrologers and the Spiritualists' National Union.

Patsy runs www.astrocast.com.au, www.patsybennett.com, facebook @patsybennettpsychicastrology and insta@patsybennettastrology.

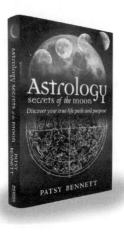

Available online at www.rockpoolpublishing.co or at all good book stores.

Further reading of astronomical data

Michelsen, Neil F. and Pottenger, Rique (1997), *The American Ephemeris for the 21st Century 2000 to 2050 at Midnight*, ACS Publications.

COMPUTER PROGRAMS OF ASTRONOMICAL DATA

Solar Fire, Esoteric Technologies Pty Ltd.